Level 5

Retold by G. C. Thornley
Series Editors: Andy Hopkins and Jocelyn Potter

Pearson Education Limited

Edinburgh Gate, Harlow,
Essex CM20 2JE, England
and Associated Companies throughout the world.

ISBN: 978-1-4058-8239-2

First published in the Longman Simplified English Series 1960
First published in the Longman Fiction Series 1993
This compilation first published 1997
First published by Penguin Books Ltd 1999
This edition first published 2008

3 5 7 9 10 8 6 4 2

We are grateful to the following for permission to reproduce simplified versions
of copyright material: the Estate of H. E. Bates for "Silas the Good" from My Uncle
Silas by H. E. Bates; A. P. Watt Ltd on behalf of the Royal Literary Fund for "Mabel"
by W. Somerset Maugham from The Gentleman in the Parlour, published by William
Heinemann Ltd/Doubleday & Co. Inc.; the William Saroyan Foundation for "The
Barber's Uncle" by William Saroyan from The Barber's Uncle, published by Faber &
Faber Ltd; Laurence Pollinger Limited and the Estate of Frieda Lawrence Ravagli for the
"The Rocking-Horse Winner" from The Complete Short Stories of D. H. Lawrence,
published by William Heinemann Ltd.

Text copyright © Pearson Education Ltd 2008
Illustrations by David Frankland

The moral rights of the authors have been asserted

Typeset by Graphicraft Ltd, Hong Kong
Set in 11/14pt Bembo
Printed in China
SWTC/02

Published by Pearson Education Ltd in association with
Penguin Books Ltd, both companies being subsidiaries of Pearson Plc

For a complete list of the titles available in the Penguin Readers series please write to your local
Pearson Longman office or to: Penguin Readers Marketing Department, Pearson Education,
Edinburgh Gate, Harlow, Essex CM20 2JE, England.

Contents

Introduction

In a short time Sarah forced back her tears. The cards must be typed. But still in a faint, golden light from her dandelion dream, she fingered the typewriter keys absently for a little while, her mind and heart on the country walk with her young farmer. But soon she came back to the streets of Manhattan, and the typewriter began to jump.

Many of the stories in this collection are about ordinary people living ordinary lives, just like Sarah in the paragraph above from O. Henry's story 'Springtime on the Menu'. What could be more ordinary than a young typist dreaming about her summer love? Or a man's embarrassment at trying to open a bank account for the first time, as in Stephen Leacock's 'My Bank Account'. Some of the stories are light-hearted and humorous, others are darker and more serious, while 'The Rocking-Horse Winner' and 'The Upper Berth' take us into worlds of mystery and magic.

This collection brings together the work of a number of well-known British and American writers. Some of those included here, like D. H. Lawrence and Mark Twain, are better known for their full-length novels. Others, like O. Henry and H. H. Munro, are remembered mainly for their short stories.

The writers come from very different backgrounds, and their different experiences and points of view are clear from their writing. Herbert Ernest Bates (1905–74) worked as a lawyer's clerk before becoming a writer. He wrote more than thirty books, including the popular and well-known *The Darling Buds of May* (1958, also a Penguin Reader), as well as plays and some wonderful collections of short stories. Many of his stories take people and places in the English countryside as their subject matter. 'Silas The Good' is typical of the best of his stories; it paints a gentle, humorous picture of a country character.

The writer William Somerset Maugham (1874–1965) was born in Paris to an Irish family. His mother died when he was eight. After his father's death two years later, he was sent to England to live with an uncle. Maugham studied medicine in Germany and England before deciding to become a writer. During the First World War he developed a love of travelling that stayed with him for the rest of his life. One of his best known novels is *Of Human Bondage* (1915), and his excellent short stories show one of the strengths of a true short-story writer – the ability to attract the reader's attention quickly and keep it to the end.

William Saroyan (1908–81) was born in California to an Armenian family. Many of his stories, including 'The Barber's Uncle', contain Armenian characters and describe their joy for life despite their difficulties. Saroyan wrote a large number of short stories, many of which appeared first in magazines and then later in book form. He also wrote for the stage.

David Herbert Lawrence (1885–1930) was one of the greatest English writers of his time. Brought up in a family where his father was a coal miner and his mother a schoolteacher, he was in a good position to observe the English class divisions that are often a feature of his writing. Lawrence also wrote poems, many of them based on his own experiences while he was on his travels in Europe and the United States.

O. Henry is the pen name of the American short-story writer William Sydney Porter (1862–1910). After leaving school at the age of fifteen, Porter worked in a bank. He then spent some time in prison for stealing money, and he gained many of his ideas from conversations with other prisoners. His stories tell of the lives of ordinary people and often have a surprising twist in the ending – in 'Springtime on the Menu' the ending is a happy one, full of hope for the future.

The English writer Hector Hugh Munro (1870–1916) also wrote under the pen name of Saki. He lived for some time in Burma, Russia and France before settling in London. At the beginning of the First World War, at the age of forty-four, he joined the army and was killed in action. He wrote books and plays, but is best known for his clever and amusing short stories.

Samuel Langhorne Clements (1835–1910) wrote under the pen name of Mark Twain, and is one of America's best known storytellers. He grew up near the Mississippi, and for some years worked as a steamship pilot on the river before becoming a writer. His most famous works are *The Adventures of Tom Sawyer* (1876), which is also a Penguin Reader, and *The Adventures of Huckleberry Finn* (1884), which is in the Penguin Active Reading series.

Francis Marion Crawford (1854–1909) is best known for his ghost stories, of which 'The Upper Berth', a mystery set on board a ship, is a good example. He was born in Italy to American parents, was educated in the United States and Europe, and worked for some time for a newspaper in India. Many of his stories are set in India.

Stephen Butler Laycock (1869–1944) was an English-born Canadian economist and writer. He studied in Toronto and Chicago, and taught in the Department of Economics and Political Science at McGill University. Although he wrote about these subjects as well as producing two books on the lives of famous people, he is best known for his collections of humorous short stories. He also wrote a book about his own life, *The Boy I Left Behind Me* (1946).

The stories in this collection are very different from each other, and entertaining. Most end happily and many have an unexpected twist at the end. All of them have that most important feature for a successful short story – they catch the reader's attention from the start.

Silas The Good *H. E. Bates*

In a life of 95 years, my Uncle Silas found time to try most things, and there was a time when he became a gravedigger.

The churchyard at Solbrook stands a long way outside the village on a little hill above the river valley. And there, dressed in a blue shirt and old brown trousers, my Uncle Silas used to dig perhaps one grave a month.

He worked all day there at the blue-brown clay, with no one for company except birds picking the worms out of the thrown-up earth. Small and ugly, he looked like a stone figure that had dropped off the roof of the little church, someone who had lived too long and might go on living and digging the graves of others for ever.

He was digging a grave there once on the south side of the churchyard on a sweet, hot day in May, the grass already long and deep, with golden flowers rising everywhere among the gravestones.

By midday he was fairly well down with the grave, and had fixed his boards to the sides. The spring had been very dry and cold, but now, in the shelter of the grave, in the strong sun, it seemed like midsummer. It was so good that Silas sat in the bottom of the grave and had his dinner, eating his bread and meat, and washing it down with the cold tea he always carried in a beer bottle. After eating, he began to feel sleepy, and finally he went to sleep there, at the bottom of the grave, with his wet, ugly mouth falling open and the beer bottle in one hand resting on his knee.

He had been asleep for 15 or 20 minutes when he woke up and saw someone standing at the top of the grave, looking down at him. At first he thought it was a woman. Then he saw his

1

mistake. It was a female. He was too surprised to say anything, and the female stood looking down at him, very angry at something, making holes in the grass with a large umbrella. She was very pale and thin, with a round, unattractive face. She seemed to have a pair of men's boots on below her thick, black skirt.

He did not have time to take another look before she attacked him. She waved her umbrella and shouted, criticizing his laziness, stupidity and disrespect.

She shook her head from side to side and stamped one of her feet. Finally she demanded to know, her thin neck stretching down at him, why he was drinking beer down there on holy ground, in a place of rest for the dead.

Now at the best of times it was difficult for my Uncle Silas, with his full red lips, red eyes and nose, not to look like a drunken sailor. But there was only one thing that he drank when he was working, and that was cold tea. It was true that the tea always had a little alcohol in it, but even so, it was mainly cold tea.

Silas let the female talk for almost five minutes, and then he raised his hat and said, 'Good afternoon, madam. Aren't the flowers nice?'

'Not satisfied with your disrespectful behaviour on holy ground,' she said, 'you're drunk, too!'

'No, madam,' he said. 'I wish I was.'

'Beer!' she said. 'Couldn't you leave the beer alone here, of all places?'

Silas held up the beer bottle. 'Madam,' he said, 'what's in here wouldn't harm a fly. It wouldn't harm you.'

'It is responsible for the ruin of thousands of homes all over England!' she said.

'Cold tea,' Silas said.

She gave a cry of anger and stamped her foot. 'Cold tea!'

'Yes, madam. Cold tea.' Silas opened the bottle and held it up to her. 'Try it, madam. Try it if you don't believe me.'

'Thank you. Not out of that bottle.'

'All right. I've got a cup,' Silas said. He looked in his dinner basket and found a metal cup. He filled it with tea and held it up to her. 'Try it, madam. Try it. It won't hurt you.'

'Well!' she said, and she reached down for the cup. She took it and touched it with her thin lips. 'Well, it's certainly some sort of tea.'

'Just ordinary tea, madam,' Silas said. 'Made this morning. You're not drinking it. Take a good drink.'

She took a real drink then, washing it round her mouth.

'Good, isn't it?' Silas said.

'Yes,' she said, 'it's very nice.'

'Drink it up,' he said. 'Have a little more. I suppose you've walked a long way?'

'Yes,' she said, 'I'm afraid I have. All the way from Bedford. Rather further than I thought. I'm not as young as I used to be.'

'Nonsense,' Silas said. 'Young? You look twenty.' He took his coat and spread it on the new earth above the grave. 'Sit down and rest yourself, madam. Sit down and look at the flowers.'

Rather to his surprise, she sat down. She took another drink of the tea and said, 'I think I'll unpin my hat.' She took off her hat and held it on her knees.

'Young?' Silas said. 'Madam, you're just a chicken. Wait until you're as old as I am, and then you can begin to talk. I can remember the Crimean War!'★

'Really?' she said. 'You must have had a full and interesting life.'

'Yes, madam.'

She smiled weakly, for the first time. 'I am sorry I spoke as I

★Crimean War: a war (1853–56) between Russia on one side and Turkey, Britain, France and Sardinia on the other.

3

did. It upset me to think of anyone drinking in this place.'

'That's all right, madam,' Silas said. 'I haven't touched a drop of alcohol for years. I used to. I've not always been as good.'

Old Silas reached up to her with the bottle and said, 'Have some more, madam,' and she held out the cup until it was full again. 'Thank you,' she said. She looked quite pleasant now, softened by the tea and the smell of flowers and the sun on her head. Somehow she stopped looking like a female and became a woman.

'But you're a better man now?' she said.

'Yes, madam,' Silas said, with a slight shake of his head, as if he were a man in real sorrow. 'Yes, madam, I'm a better man now.'

'It was a long fight against the drink?'

'A long fight, madam? Yes, it was a very long fight.' He raised his hat a little.

'How long?' she said.

'Well, madam,' said Silas, settling back in the grave, where he had been sitting all that time, 'I was born in hungry times. Bad times, madam, very bad times. The food and the water were bad. Very bad. There was disease too. So we had beer, madam. Everybody had beer. The babies had beer. I've been fighting against it for 80 years and more.'

'And now you've beaten it?'

'Yes, madam,' said my Uncle Silas, who had drunk more in 80 years than there is water in the Thames. 'I've beaten it.' He held up the beer bottle. 'Nothing but cold tea. You'll have some more cold tea, madam, won't you?'

'It's very kind of you,' she said.

So Silas poured out another cup of the cold tea and she sat on the graveside and drank it in the sunshine, becoming all the time more and more human.

'And it wasn't surprising,' as Silas told me afterwards. 'It was still my winter tea that we were drinking. You see, I had a

4

summer tea with only a little alcohol in it, and I had a winter tea with nearly a cupful in it. The weather had been cold up to that day, and I hadn't changed from winter to summer tea.'

They sat there for about another half an hour, drinking the cold tea, and during that time there was nothing she did not hear about my Uncle Silas's life: not only how he had left the beer and was trying to give up the bad language, but how he had given up the ladies and the horses and the doubtful stories and the lying and everything else that a man can give up.

As he finally climbed up out of the grave to shake hands with her and say good afternoon, she must have believed that he was a very pure and religious man.

Except that her face was very red, she walked away as proudly as she had come. That was the last he ever saw of her. But that afternoon, on the 2.45 train out of Solbrook, there was a woman with a large umbrella in one hand and a bunch of golden flowers in the other. In the warm, crowded train there was a smell of something stronger than cold tea. The woman appeared to be a little excited, and to everyone's embarrassment she talked a great deal.

Her subject was someone she had met that afternoon.

'A good man,' she told them. 'A good man.'

Mabel   *W. Somerset Maugham*

I was at Pagan, in Burma, and from there I took the steamship to Mandalay, but two days before I got there, when the boat was tied up for the night at a riverside village, I made up my mind to go on shore. The captain told me that there was a pleasant little club where I could go and be comfortable; they were quite used to having strangers arrive like that from the ship, and the secretary was a very nice man; I might even get a game of cards. I had nothing in the world to do, so I got into one of the carts that were waiting at the landing stage and was driven to the club.

There was a man sitting outside, and as I walked up he welcomed me and asked me what kind of drink I would like. He never considered the possibility that I might not want any kind of drink at all. I chose one and sat down. He was a tall, thin man, browned by the sun. I never knew his name, but when we had been talking for a short time another man came in, who told me he was the secretary. He called my friend George.

'Have you heard from your wife yet?' he asked him.

The other's eyes brightened.

'Yes, a letter arrived today. She's having a nice time.'

'Did she tell you not to worry?'

George gave a little laugh, but was I mistaken in thinking that there was in it a sound of sorrow?

'In fact she did. But that's easier said than done. Of course I know she wants a holiday, and I'm glad she's having one, but it's hard on me.' He turned to me. 'You see, this is the first time I've ever been separated from my wife, and I'm like a lost dog without her.'

'How long have you been married?'

'Five minutes.'

The secretary of the club laughed.

'Don't be a fool, George. You've been married for eight years.'

After we had talked a little, George, looking at his watch, said he must go and change his clothes for dinner and left us. The secretary watched him disappear into the night with a smile that was not unkind.

'We all talk to him as much as we can, now that he's alone,' he told me. 'He's so terribly unhappy since his wife went home.'

'It must be very pleasant for her to know that her husband loves her as much as that.'

'Mabel is an unusual kind of woman.'

He called the boy and ordered more drinks. These generous people did not ask you if you would have anything; they simply ordered you one. Then he settled himself in his chair, lit a cigarette and told me the story of George and Mabel.

George asked her to marry him when he was on holiday in England, and she accepted him; and when he returned to Burma, it was arranged that she should join him in six months. But one difficulty came after another – Mabel's father died, the war came, George was sent to an area unsuitable for a white woman – so that in the end it was seven years before she was able to start. He made all the arrangements for the marriage, which would take place on the day of her arrival, and went down to Rangoon to meet her. On the morning on which the ship was supposed to arrive he borrowed a motor car and drove along to meet it.

Then, suddenly, without warning, he was afraid. He had not seen Mabel for seven years. He had forgotten what she was like. She was a total stranger. He felt a terrible sinking in his stomach, and his knees began to shake. He couldn't do it. He must tell Mabel that he was very sorry, but he couldn't, he really couldn't marry her. But how could a man tell a girl a thing like that when she had been expecting to marry him for seven years and had come 6,000 miles to do it? He couldn't do that either. George was seized with a courage brought on by hopelessness. There was a boat there just about to start for Singapore; he wrote a hurried letter to Mabel and, without any luggage at all, just in the clothes he stood up in, he jumped on board.

The letter that Mabel received was something like this:

Dearest Mabel,

I have been suddenly called away on business and do not know when I shall be back. I think it would be much wiser if you returned to England. My plans are very uncertain.

Your loving
GEORGE.

But when he arrived at Singapore he found a telegram waiting for him.

QUITE UNDERSTAND. DON'T WORRY. LOVE. MABEL.

Fear made him think quickly.

'Good heavens, I believe she's following me,' he said.

He got in touch with the shipping office at Rangoon and, sure enough, her name was on the passenger list of the ship that was now on its way to Singapore. There was not a moment to lose. He jumped on the train to Bangkok. But he was anxious; she would have no difficulty in finding out that he had gone to Bangkok and it was just as simple for her to take the train as it had been for him. Fortunately there was a French ship sailing next day for Saigon. He took it. At Saigon he would be safe; she would never imagine that he had gone there; and if she did, surely by now she would have understood.

It is five days' journey from Bangkok to Saigon and the boat is dirty, crowded and uncomfortable. He was glad to arrive, and he drove to the hotel. He signed his name in the visitors' book and a telegram was immediately handed to him. It contained only two words: LOVE. MABEL. They were enough to make him shake with fear.

'When is the next boat for Hong Kong?' he asked.

Now his escape grew serious. He sailed to Hong Kong but dared not stay there; he went to Manila, but Manila seemed to threaten him; he went on to Shanghai. Shanghai made him anxious; every time he went out of the hotel he expected to run straight into Mabel's arms – no, Shanghai did not suit him at all. The only thing was to go to Yokohama. At the Grand Hotel at Yokohama a telegram was waiting for him.

SO SORRY TO HAVE MISSED YOU AT MANILA. LOVE. MABEL.

He examined the shipping news feverishly. Where was she now? He went back to Shanghai. This time he went straight to the club and asked for a telegram. It was handed to him.

ARRIVING SOON. LOVE. MABEL.

No, no, he was not so easy to catch as that. He had already made his plans. The Yangtse is a long river and the Yangtse was falling. He could just catch the last ship that could get him up to Chungking and then no one could travel until the following spring except in a smaller boat. A journey like that in a smaller boat was impossible for a woman alone. He went to Hankow and from Hankow to Ichang, he changed boats here and from Ichang went to Chungking. But he was not going to take any risks now: there was a place called Cheng-tu, the capital of Szechuan, and it was four hundred miles away. It could only be reached by road, and the road was full of robbers. A man would be safe there.

George collected chair-bearers and servants and set out. It was with great relief that he saw at last the walls of the lonely Chinese city. From those walls at sunset you could see the snowy mountains of Tibet.

He could rest at last: Mabel would never find him there. By chance the consul was a friend of his and he stayed with him. He enjoyed the comfort of a fine house, he enjoyed his rest after that tiring escape across Asia, and above all he enjoyed his feeling of safety. The weeks passed lazily one after the other.

One morning George and the consul were in the courtyard looking at some strange old objects that a Chinese man had brought for their examination when there was a loud knocking at the great door of the consul's house. The doorman threw it open. A chair carried by four men entered and was put down. Mabel stepped out. She was neat and calm and fresh. There was nothing in her appearance to suggest that she had just come in after two weeks on the road. George was turned to stone. He was as pale as death. She went up to him.

'Hello, George, I was so afraid I had missed you again.'

'Hello, Mabel,' he said in a trembling voice.

He did not know what to say. He looked this way and that: she stood between him and the doorway. She looked at him with a smile in her blue eyes.

'You haven't changed at all,' she said. 'Men can change so much in seven years and I was afraid you'd got fat and had lost your hair. I've been so nervous. It would have been terrible if after all these years I simply hadn't been able to make myself marry you after all.'

She turned to George's host. 'Are you the consul?' she asked.

'I am.'

'If you are the consul, you can marry us. I'm ready to marry him as soon as I've had a bath.'

And she did.

The Barber's Uncle   *William Saroyan*

Miss Gamma said I needed a haircut, my mother said I needed a haircut, my brother Krikor said I needed a haircut: the whole world wanted me to get a haircut. My head was too big for the world. Too much black hair, the world said.

Everybody said, 'When are you going to get a haircut?'

There was a big businessman in our town named Huntingdon who used to buy an evening paper from me every day. He was a man who weighed 240 pounds, owned two Cadillacs, a lot of land, and had over a million dollars in the Valley Bank, as well as a small head, without hair, right on top of him where everybody could see it. He used to make railroad men from out of town walk a long way to see my head. 'There's California for you,' he used to shout in the street. 'There's good weather and health. There's hair on a head,' he used to shout.

Miss Gamma was bitter about the size of my head.

'I'm not mentioning any names,' she said one day, 'but unless a certain young man in this class visits a barber one of these days and has his hair cut, he will be sent to a worse place than this.'

She didn't mention any names. All she did was look at me.

'What's the big idea?' my brother Krikor said.

I was glad the world was angry with me, but one day a small bird tried to build a nest in my hair, so I hurried up town to a barber.

◆

I was sleeping on the grass under the tree in our yard when a bird flew down from the tree and started making its way into my hair. It was a warm winter day and the world was sleeping. It was very still everywhere in the world. Nobody was rushing round in a car

11

and the only thing you could hear was the warm and cold, happy and sad silence of reality.

The world. Ah, it was good to be alive somewhere. It was wonderful to have a small house in the world. Rooms and tables and chairs and beds. Pictures on the walls. It was strange and wonderful to be somewhere in the world. Alive, able to move through time and space, any time of the day and night: to breathe and eat and laugh and talk and sleep and grow. To see and hear and touch. To walk through the places of the world under the sun. To be in the world.

I was glad the world was there, so I could be there too. I was alone, so I was sad about everything, but I was glad too. I was so glad about everything that I was sad. I wanted to dream about it: the places I had never seen. The wonderful cities of the world: New York, London, Paris, Berlin, Vienna, Constantinople, Rome, Cairo. The streets, the houses, the people alive. The doors and windows everywhere. And the trains at night, and the ships at sea. The dark sad sea. And the bright moments of all the dead years, the cities buried under time, the places decayed and gone. Ah, in 1919 I dreamed a dream one day: I dreamed the living lived for ever. I dreamed the end of change and decay and death.

Then the bird flew down from the tree to my head and tried to build a nest in my hair, and I woke up.

I opened my eyes but didn't move.

I had no idea the bird was in my hair until it began to sing. I had never before in my life heard the cry of a bird so clearly, and what I heard sounded very new, and at the same time very natural and old. There had been no sound in the world and then suddenly I had heard the bird.

Then I realized that such a thing was not proper. It was not proper for a small bird to be in anybody's hair.

So I jumped up and hurried to town, and the bird, properly frightened, flew as far away as it could go in one breath.

12

The world was right. Miss Gamma was right. My brother Krikor was right. The thing to do was to get a haircut, so birds wouldn't try to build nests in your hair.

There was an Armenian barber on Mariposa Street named Aram who was really a farmer, or perhaps a teacher. I didn't know. I only knew he had a little shop on Mariposa Street and spent most of his time reading Armenian papers, rolling cigarettes, smoking them, and watching the people go by. I never did see him giving anybody a haircut, although I suppose one or two people went into his shop by mistake.

I went to Aram's shop on Mariposa Street and woke him up. He was sitting at the little table with an Armenian book open in front of him, sleeping.

In Armenian I said, 'Will you cut my hair? I have twenty-five cents.'

'Ah,' he said, 'I am glad to see you. What is your name? Sit down. I will make coffee first. Ah, that is a fine head of hair you have.'

'Everybody wants me to get a haircut,' I said.

'That is the way with the world,' he said. 'Always telling you what to do. What's wrong with a little hair? Why do they do it? Earn money, they say. Buy a farm. This. That. Ah, they are against letting a man live a quiet life.'

'Can you do it?' I said. 'Can you cut it all away so they will not talk about it again for a long time?'

'Coffee,' said the barber. 'Let us drink a little coffee first.'

He brought me a cup of coffee, and I wondered how it was I had never before visited him, perhaps the most interesting man in the whole city. I knew he was an unusual man from the way he woke when I entered the store, from the way he talked and walked. He was about fifty and I was eleven. He was no taller than I was and no heavier, but his face was the face of a man who has found out the truth, who knows, who is wise, but who loves everything and is not unkind.

When he opened his eyes, his look seemed to say, 'The world? I know all about the world. Evil and hatred and fear. But I love it all.'

I lifted the small cup to my lips and drank the hot black liquid. It tasted finer than anything I had ever tasted before.

'Sit down,' he said in Armenian. 'Sit down, sit down. We have nowhere to go. We have nothing to do. Your hair will not grow in an hour.'

I sat down and laughed in Armenian, and he began to tell me about the world.

He told me about his Uncle Misak who was born in Moush.

We drank the coffee, and then I got into the chair and he began to cut my hair. He gave me the worst of all haircuts but he told me about his poor Uncle Misak and the tiger. I went out of his shop with a very bad haircut, but I didn't care about that. He wasn't a real barber. He was just pretending to be a barber, so his wife wouldn't worry him too much. He was just doing that to satisfy the world. All he wanted to do was read and talk to good people. He had five children, three boys and two girls, but they were all like his wife, and he couldn't talk to them. All they wanted to know was how much money he was making.

'My poor Uncle Misak,' he said to me, 'was born a long time ago in Moush and he was a very wild boy, although he was not a thief. He could fight any two boys in the whole city, and if necessary their fathers and mothers at the same time. Their grandfathers and grandmothers too.

'So everybody said to my poor Uncle Misak, "Misak, you are strong; why don't you earn money by fighting?" So he did. He broke the bones of eighteen strong men before he was twenty. And all he did with his money was eat and drink and give the rest to children. He didn't want money.

'Ah,' the barber said, 'that was long ago. Now everybody wants

14

money. They told him he would be sorry some day, and of course they were right. They told him to take care of his money because some day he would no longer be strong and he would have no money. And the day came. My poor Uncle Misak was forty years old and no longer strong, and he had no money. They laughed at him and he went away. He went to Constantinople. Then he went to Vienna.'

'Vienna?' I said. 'Your Uncle Misak went to Vienna?'

'Yes, of course,' said the barber. 'My poor Uncle Misak went to many places. In Vienna,' he said, 'my poor uncle could not find work, and he nearly died of hunger, but did he steal so much as a loaf of bread? No, he stole nothing. Then he went to Berlin. There, too, my poor Uncle Misak nearly died of hunger.'

He was cutting my hair, left and right. I could see the black hair on the floor and feel my head becoming colder and colder. And smaller and smaller. 'Ah, Berlin,' he said. 'Cruel city of the world, streets and streets and houses and houses and people and people, but not one door for my poor Uncle Misak, not one room, not one table, not one friend.'

'Ah,' I said, 'this loneliness of man in the world. This terrible loneliness of the living.'

'And,' said the barber, 'it was the same in Paris, the same in London, the same in New York, the same in South America. It was the same everywhere, streets and streets, houses and houses, doors and doors, but no place in the world for my poor Uncle Misak.'

'Ah, God,' I prayed. 'Protect him. Father in heaven, protect him.'

'In China,' said the barber, 'my poor Uncle Misak met an Arab who worked in a French travelling show. The Arab and my Uncle Misak talked together in Turkish. The Arab said, "Brother, are you a lover of men and animals?" And my Uncle Misak said, "Brother, I love everything in God's world. Men and animals and fish and birds and rock and fire and water and everything seen and unseen." And the Arab said, "Brother, can you love even a tiger, a wild tiger?" And my Uncle Misak said, "Brother, my love for the animal is without limit." Ah, my Uncle Misak was an unhappy man.

'The Arab was very glad to hear about my uncle's love for wild animals, for he too was a very brave man. "Brother," he said to my uncle, "could you love a tiger enough to place your head into its open mouth?" '

'Protect him, God,' I prayed.

'And,' said Aram the barber, 'my Uncle Misak said, "Brother, I could." And the Arab said, "Will you join our show? Yesterday the tiger carelessly closed its mouth around the head of poor Simon Perigord, and now we have nobody with such great love for the creatures of God." My poor Uncle Misak was tired of the world, and he said, "Brother, I will join the show and place my head into the open mouth of God's holy tiger ten times a day" "That is not necessary," said the Arab. "Twice a day will be enough." So my poor Uncle Misak joined the French travelling show in China and began placing his head into the open mouth of the tiger.

'The show,' said the barber, 'travelled from China to India, from India to Afghanistan, from Afghanistan to Persia, and there, in Persia, it happened. The tiger and my poor Uncle Misak became very good friends. In Teheran, in that old city, the tiger grew wild again. It was a very hot day. The tiger felt very angry and ran around all day. My poor Uncle Misak placed his head into the open mouth of the tiger in Teheran, that ugly city of Persia, and he was about to take his head out of the tiger's mouth when the tiger, full of the ugliness of things living on the earth, closed its jaws.'

I got out of the chair and saw a strange person in the mirror – myself. I was frightened and all my hair was gone. I paid Aram, the barber, twenty-five cents and went home. Everybody laughed at me. My brother Krikor said he had never seen such a bad haircut before.

But it was all right.

All I could think about for weeks was the barber's poor Uncle Misak, whose head was bitten off by the tiger, and I looked forward to the day when I would need a haircut again, so I could go to Aram's shop and listen to his story of man on earth, lost and lonely and always in danger, the sad story of his poor Uncle Misak. The sad story of every man alive.

The Rocking-Horse Winner   *D. H. Lawrence*

There was a woman who was beautiful, who started with all the advantages, but who had no luck. She married for love, and the love turned to dust. She had lovely children, but she felt that they had been forced on her, and she could not love them. They looked at her coldly, as if they were finding fault with her, and she felt that she must cover up some fault in herself. But she never knew what she must cover up. But when her children were present, she always felt the centre of her heart go hard. This troubled her, and in her manner she was more gentle and anxious for her children, as if she loved them very much. Only she herself knew that at the centre of her heart was a hard little place that could not feel love, no, not for anybody. Everybody else always said of her, 'She is such a good mother. She loves her children.' Only she herself, and her children themselves, knew that it was not true. They read it in each other's eyes.

There were a boy and two little girls. They lived in a pleasant house, with a garden, and they had servants, and they felt themselves to be better than anyone in the neighbourhood.

Although they lived like rich people, they felt an anxiety in the house. There was never enough money. The mother had a small income, and the father had a small income, but it was not nearly enough for the social position which they had to keep up. The father went into town to some office. But though he had good hopes of a better position, those hopes were never realized. There was never enough money, but the way of life was always kept up.

Finally the mother said, 'I will see if *I* can do something.' But she did not know where to begin. She thought as hard as she could, and tried this thing and the other, but could not find anything successful. The failure brought deep lines to her face. Her children were growing up, they would have to go to school. There must be more money, there must be more money. The father, who was always very good-looking and expensive in his tastes, seemed as if he never *would* be able to do anything worth doing. And the mother, who had a great belief in herself, did not succeed any better, and her tastes were just as expensive.

And so a whisper began to fill the house, though it was never spoken: *There must be more money! There must be more money!* The children could hear it all the time, though nobody said it out loud. They heard it in their own room, which was full of expensive and wonderful toys. Behind the shining modern rocking horse a voice whispered: 'There *must* be more money! There *must* be more money!' And the children stopped playing, to listen for a moment. They looked into each other's eyes, to see if they had all heard. And each one saw in the eyes of the other two that they too had heard. 'There *must* be more money!'

It came whispering from the springs of the rocking horse – and even the horse, bending its wooden head, heard it. The other toys heard it, and even the foolish little dog looked more foolish because he heard the secret whisper all over the house: 'There must be more money!'

But nobody ever said it out loud. The whisper was everywhere, and therefore no one spoke it. Just as no one ever says: 'We are breathing!' although breath is coming and going all the time.

'Mother,' said the boy Paul one day, 'why don't we keep a car of our own? Why do we always use Uncle's, or a taxi?'

'Because we're the poor members of the family,' said the mother.

'But why *are* we, Mother?'

'Well – I suppose,' she said slowly and bitterly, 'it's because your father has no luck.'

The boy was silent for some time.

'Is luck money, Mother?' he asked, rather anxiously.

'No, Paul. Not quite. It's what causes you to have money. If you're lucky, you have money. That's why it's better to be born lucky than rich. If you're rich, you may lose your money. But if you're lucky, you will always get more money.'

'Oh! Will you? And is Father not lucky?'

'Very unlucky, I think,' she said bitterly.

The boy watched her with uncertain eyes.

'Why?' he asked.

'I don't know. Nobody ever knows why one person is lucky and another unlucky.'

'Don't they? Nobody at all? Does *nobody* know?'

'Perhaps God. But He never tells.'

'He ought to, then. But aren't you lucky either, Mother?'

'I can't be, if I married an unlucky husband.'

'But by yourself, aren't you?'

'I used to think I was, before I married. Now I think I am very unlucky.'

'Why?'

'Well – never mind! Perhaps I'm not really,' she said.

The child looked at her to see if she meant it. But he saw, by the lines of her mouth, that she was only trying to hide something from him.

'Well,' he said bravely, 'I'm a lucky person.'

'Why?' said his mother, with a sudden laugh.

'God told me,' he said.

'I hope He did, dear!' she said, again with a laugh, but a bitter one.

'He did, Mother!'

'Excellent!' said the mother, using one of her husband's words.

The boy saw that she did not believe him, and then realized that she was paying no attention to what he said. This made him angry: he wanted to force her to listen.

He went off by himself, in a childish way, in search of the secret of luck. He was busy with his thoughts, taking no notice of other people. He wanted luck, he wanted it, he wanted it. While the two girls were playing with their toys, he sat on his big rocking horse, riding into space with a madness that made the little girls look at him anxiously. Wildly the horse flew, the wavy dark hair of the boy was thrown up into the air, his eyes had a strange look in them. The little girls dared not speak to him.

When he had ridden to the end of his mad little journey, he climbed down and stood in front of his rocking horse, his eyes fixed on its lowered face. Its red mouth was slightly open, its big eye was wide and bright like glass.

'Now!' he silently commanded the horse. 'Now, take me to where there is luck! Now take me!'

And he struck the horse on the neck with the little whip he had asked Uncle Oscar for. He *knew* the horse could take him to where there was luck, if only he forced it. So he got on again, and started on his wild ride, hoping finally to get there. He knew he could get there.

'You'll break your horse, Paul!' said the nurse.

'He's always riding like that! I wish he'd stop!' said his older sister Joan.

But he only looked down at them in angry silence. The nurse did not know what to do with him. In any case, he was growing too old for her to control.

One day his mother and his Uncle Oscar came in when he was on one of his wild rides. He did not speak to them.

'Hello!' said his uncle. 'Riding a winner?'

'Aren't you growing too big for a rocking horse? You're not a little boy any longer, you know,' said his mother.

But Paul only gave her a angry blue look. He never spoke to anybody when he was riding like this. His mother watched him with an anxious expression on her face.

At last he suddenly stopped forcing his horse backwards and forwards, and slid down.

'Well, I got there,' he said, his blue eyes still angry and his long legs apart.

'Where did you get to?' asked his mother.

'Where I wanted to go,' he cried angrily.

'That's right!' said Uncle Oscar. 'Don't stop until you get there. What's the horse's name?'

'He doesn't have a name,' said the boy.

'Does he get on all right without a name?' asked the uncle.

'Well, he has different names. He was called Sansovino last week.'

'Sansovino? That won a race. The Ascot. How did you know his name?'

'He always talks about horse races with Bassett,' said Joan.

The uncle was pleased to find that the boy knew all the racing news. Bassett, the young gardener, who had been wounded in the left foot in the war and had got his present work with the help of Oscar Creswell, was the perfect man for news of racing. He lived in the world of racing news, and the small boy lived there with him.

Oscar Creswell had a talk with Bassett.

'Master Paul comes and asks me, so I have to tell him, sir,' said Bassett, his face terribly serious, as if he were speaking of religious matters.

'And does he ever risk money on a horse he likes?'

'Well – I don't want to tell. Would you mind asking him himself? He takes a pleasure in it, and perhaps he wouldn't like me to talk of it, sir, if you don't mind.' Bassett was as serious as a church.

The uncle went back to the boy and took him off for a ride in his car.

'Say, Paul, do you ever put money on a horse?' the uncle asked.

The boy watched the good-looking man closely.

'Why? Do you think I oughtn't to?' he asked.

'Not at all! I thought perhaps you could tell me which horse would win the Lincoln.'

The car sped on into the country, going to Uncle George's place in Hampshire.

'Honestly?' said the boy.

'Honestly!' said the uncle.

'Well, then, Daffodil will win that race.'

'Daffodil! I doubt it, Paul. What about Mirza?'

'I only know the winner,' said the boy. 'That's Daffodil.'

'Daffodil!'

There was a pause. Daffodil was not a well-known horse.

'Uncle!'

'Yes?'

'You won't tell anyone else, will you? I promised Bassett.'

'Why Bassett?'

'We're partners. We've been partners from the beginning. Uncle, he lent me my first five shillings, which I lost. I promised him that only he and I would know. But you gave me that ten-shilling note I started winning with, so I thought you were lucky. You won't tell anyone else, will you?'

The boy looked straight at his uncle from his big, hot, blue eyes. The uncle laughed anxiously.

'All right, Paul. I'll keep Daffodil's name a secret. How much are you risking on him?'

'All except twenty pounds,' said the boy. 'I keep that safe.'

The uncle thought it a good joke.

'You keep twenty pounds back, do you, young man? How much are you betting, then?'

'I'm betting three hundred,' said the boy seriously. 'But you mustn't tell anyone, Uncle Oscar.'

The uncle burst out laughing.

'I won't tell anyone,' he said, laughing. 'But where's your three hundred?'

'Bassett keeps it for me. We're partners.'

'And what is Bassett putting on Daffodil?'

'He won't put quite as much as I do, I expect. Perhaps he'll bet a hundred and fifty.'

'What? Pennies?' laughed the uncle.

'Pounds,' said the child, with a surprised look at his uncle. 'Bassett keeps a bigger amount back than I do.'

Between wonder and amusement Uncle Oscar was silent. He said no more of the matter, but he decided that he would take the boy with him to the Lincoln races, and so he did.

'Now,' he said, 'I'm putting twenty pounds on Mirza, and I'll put five for you on any horse you like. Which do you choose?'

'Daffodil, Uncle.'

'No, not five pounds on Daffodil!'

'I would if it was my own money,' said the child.

'Good! Good! Five for me and five for you on Daffodil.'

The child had never been to a race meeting before, and his eyes were blue fire. He closed his lips tight and watched. A Frenchman just in front had put his money on Lancelot. Wild with excitement, he waved his arms up and down, shouting, 'Lancelot! Lancelot!'

Daffodil came in first, Lancelot second, Mirza third. The child, with red face and eyes flaming, was strangely calm. His uncle brought him the four five-pound notes which he had won.

'What shall I do with these?' he cried, waving them in front of the boy's eyes.

'I suppose we'll talk to Bassett,' said the boy. 'I expect I have fifteen hundred pounds now, the twenty I keep back and this twenty.'

His uncle studied him for some moments.

'Listen,' he said. 'You're not serious about Bassett and that fifteen hundred pounds, are you?'

'Yes, I am. But you mustn't tell anyone, Uncle.'

'Very well. But I must talk to Bassett.'

'If you'd like to be a partner, Uncle, with Bassett and me, we could all be partners. Only you'd have to promise, on your honour, not to tell anyone else. Bassett and I are lucky, and you must be lucky, because it was your ten shillings that I started winning with . . .'

Uncle Oscar took both Bassett and Paul into Richmond Park for an afternoon, and there they talked.

'It's like this, you see, sir,' Bassett said. 'Master Paul made me talk about racing events, telling stories, you know, sir. And he always wanted to know if I'd won or lost. It's about a year ago now that I put five shillings on Blush of Dawn for him; and we lost. Then the luck turned, with that ten shillings he had from you. We put that money on Singhalese. And since that time, it's been fairly steady. What do you say, Master Paul?'

'We're all right when we're sure,' said Paul. 'It's when we're not quite sure that we lose.'

'Oh, but we're careful then,' said Bassett.

'But when are you *sure*?' smiled Uncle Oscar.

'It's Master Paul, sir,' said Bassett, in a secretive, religious voice. 'It seems to come from heaven to him. Like Daffodil, now, for the Lincoln. That was quite sure.'

'Did you bet on Daffodil?' asked Oscar Creswell.

'Yes, sir. I made my bit.'

'And the boy?'

Bassett said nothing. He looked at Paul.

'I made twelve hundred, didn't I, Bassett? I told Uncle I was putting three hundred on Daffodil.'

'That's right,' said Bassett.

'But where's the money?' asked the uncle.

'I keep it safely locked up, sir. Master Paul can have it any minute he likes to ask for it.'

'What, fifteen hundred pounds?'

'And twenty! And *forty*, in fact, with the twenty pounds he won at the race meeting.'

'I can hardly believe it!' said the uncle.

'If Master Paul wants you to join us, sir, I think I should accept if I were you; if you'll excuse me,' said Bassett.

Oscar Creswell thought about it. 'I'll see the money,' he said.

They drove home again, and sure enough, Bassett came round to the garden-house with fifteen hundred pounds in notes.

'You see, it's all right, Uncle, when I'm *sure*! Then we bet a lot, don't we, Bassett?'

'We do that, Master Paul.'

'And when are you sure?' said the uncle, laughing.

'Oh, well, sometimes, I'm *completely* sure, as I was about Daffodil,' said the boy; 'and sometimes I have an idea; and sometimes I haven't even an idea, have I, Bassett? Then we're careful, because we usually lose.'

'And when you're sure, as you were with Daffodil, what makes you sure, Paul?'

'Oh, well, I don't know,' said the boy in a troubled voice. 'I'm sure, you know, Uncle; that's all.'

'It's as if he had it from heaven, sir,' Bassett repeated.

'It looks like that,' said the uncle.

But he became a partner. And when it was time for another race, the Leger, Paul was 'sure' about Lively Spark, which was quite an unimportant horse. The boy was determined to put a thousand pounds on the horse, Bassett put five hundred, and Oscar Creswell two hundred. Lively Spark came in first, and the betting had been ten to one against him. Paul had made ten thousand pounds.

'You see,' he said, 'I was completely sure of him.'

Even Oscar Creswell had made two thousand.

'Listen,' he said, 'this sort of thing makes me nervous.'

'It needn't, Uncle. Perhaps I shan't be sure again for a long time.'

'But what are you going to do with your money?' asked the uncle.

'Of course,' said the boy, 'I started it for Mother. She said she had no luck because Father is unlucky, so I thought if *I* was lucky, it might stop whispering.'

'What might stop whispering?'

'Our house. I *hate* our house for whispering.'

'What does it whisper?'

'Well' – the boy paused – 'I don't know. But it's always without enough money, you know, Uncle.'

'I know it. I know it.'

'You know that people send Mother bills, and orders to pay, don't you, Uncle?'

'I'm afraid I do,' said Uncle Oscar.

'And then the house whispers, like people laughing at you behind your back. It's terrible! I thought if I was lucky...'

'You might stop it,' added the uncle.

The boy watched him with big blue eyes that had a strange cold fire in them, and he said nothing.

'Well, then,' said the uncle. 'What shall we do?'

'I wouldn't like Mother to know I was lucky,' said the boy.

'Why not, Paul?'

'She'd stop me.'

'I don't think she would.'

'Oh!' – and the boy moved uncomfortably – 'I don't want her to know, Uncle.'

'All right! We'll manage it without her knowing.'

They managed it very easily. Paul, at the other's suggestion, gave five thousand pounds to his uncle, who gave it to the family lawyer, who was then to inform Paul's mother that a relation had put five thousand pounds into his hands. This sum would be paid out on the mother's birthday, a thousand pounds at a time, for the next five years.

'So she'll have a birthday present of a thousand pounds for five years,' said Uncle Oscar. 'I hope it won't make it harder for her later.'

Paul's mother had her birthday in November. The house had been whispering worse than ever recently; and in spite of his luck, Paul could not bear it. He was very anxious to see the effect of the birthday letter telling his mother about the thousand pounds.

When there were no visitors, Paul now took his meals with his parents, as he was beyond the nurse's control. His mother went into town nearly every day. She had discovered that she could design furs and dress materials, so she worked secretly with a friend who was the chief designer for an important shop. Her friend earned several thousand pounds a year, but Paul's mother only made a few hundred, and she was not satisfied. She wanted to be first in something, and she did not succeed.

She was downstairs for breakfast on the morning of her birthday. Paul watched her face as she read her letters. He recognized the lawyer's letter. As his mother read it, her face hardened and became more expressionless. Then a cold, determined look came on her mouth. She hid the letter under the pile of others, and said not a word about it.

'Didn't you have anything nice in the post for your birthday, Mother?' said Paul.

'Quite nice,' she said, her voice cold and absent.

She went away to town without saying more.

But in the afternoon Uncle Oscar appeared. He said Paul's mother had been with the lawyer a long time, asking if the whole five thousand could not be sent immediately, as she was in debt.

'What do you think, Uncle?' said the boy.

'You must decide.'

'Oh, let her have it, then. We can get some more,' said the boy.

'Don't be too sure,' said Uncle Oscar. 'A bird in the hand is worth two in the bush.'

'But I'm sure to *know* for the other races: for the Grand National; or the Lincolnshire; or the Derby. I'm sure to know for *one* of them,' said Paul.

So Uncle Oscar signed the agreement, and Paul's mother received the whole five thousand. Then something very strange happened. The voices in the house suddenly went mad: there were thousands of them. There was new furniture, and Paul had a teacher. He was *really* going to Eton, his father's school, in the following autumn. There were flowers in the winter. And still the voices in the house, behind the flowers and under the beds, cried: 'There *must* be more money! Oh, there *must* be more money. Oh, now, more than ever, there *must* be more money!'

It frightened Paul terribly. He studied his Latin and Greek, but his most important hours were spent with Bassett. The Grand National had gone by: he had not 'known', and had lost a hundred pounds. Summer was near. He was terribly anxious about the Lincoln. But even for the Lincoln he didn't 'know', and he lost fifty pounds. He became wild-eyed and strange, as if something were going to explode in him.

'Leave it alone,' said Uncle Oscar. 'Don't trouble yourself about it!' But it seemed as if the boy couldn't really hear what his uncle was saying.

'I've got to know for the Derby! I've got to know for the Derby!' the child said again and again, his big blue eyes flaming with a sort of madness.

His mother noticed how upset he was.

'You'd better go to the seaside. Wouldn't you like to go now to the seaside, instead of waiting? I think you'd better,' she said, looking down at him anxiously, her heart strangely heavy because of him.

But the child lifted his strange blue eyes.

'I can't possibly go before the Derby, Mother!' he said. 'I can't possibly!'

'Why not?' she said, her voice becoming heavy when he did not agree. 'Why not? You can still go from the seaside to see the Derby with your Uncle Oscar, if that's what you wish. There's no need for you to wait here. Besides, I think you care too much about these races. It's a bad sign. My family has been a betting family, and you won't know until you grow up how much damage it has done. But it has done damage. I shall have to send Bassett away, and ask Uncle Oscar not to talk about racing to you, unless you promise to be reasonable about it. Go away to the seaside and forget it. You're all nerves!'

'I'll do what you like, Mother, if you don't send me away until after the Derby,' the boy said.

'Send you away from where? Just from this house?'

'Yes,' he said, looking at her.

'Why, you strange child, what makes you care about this house so much, suddenly? I never knew you loved it.'

He looked at her without speaking. He had a secret within a secret, something he had not told, even to Bassett or to his Uncle Oscar.

But his mother, after standing undecided for some moments, said: 'Very well, then! Don't go to the seaside until after the Derby, if you don't wish it. But promise me you won't let your nerves go to pieces. Promise you won't think so much about horse racing and *events*, as you call them!'

'Oh, no,' said the boy carelessly. 'I won't think much about them, Mother. You needn't worry. I wouldn't worry, Mother, if I were you.'

'If you were me, and I were you,' said his mother, 'I wonder

30

what we *would* do!'

'But you know you needn't worry, Mother, don't you?' the boy repeated.

'I should be very glad to know it,' she said in a tired voice.

'Oh, well, you *can*. I mean you *ought* to know you needn't worry,' he said.

'Ought I? Then I'll think about it,' she said.

Paul's secret of secrets was his wooden horse, that which had no name. Since the nurse had gone, he had had his rocking horse taken to his own bedroom at the top of the house.

'Surely you're too big for a rocking horse!' his mother had said.

'Well, you see, Mother, until I can have a real horse, I like to have some sort of animal,' his strange answer had been.

'Do you feel he's good company for you?' she laughed.

'Oh, yes! He's very good, and he's always good company when I'm there.'

The Derby was coming nearer, and the boy grew more and more anxious. He hardly heard what was spoken to him, he was very delicate, and his eyes were really strange. His mother was worried about him. Sometimes, for half an hour, she felt a sudden anxiety about him that was almost pain. She wanted to rush straight to him, and know he was safe.

Two nights before the Derby she was at a big party in town, when one of her feelings of anxiety about her boy filled her heart until she could hardly speak. She fought with the feeling with all her strength, but it was too strong. She had to leave the dance and go downstairs to telephone her home in the country. Miss Wilmot, who took care of the children, was terribly surprised at being rung up in the night.

'Are the children all right, Miss Wilmot?'

'Oh, yes, they are quite all right.'

'Master Paul? Is he all right?'

'He was when he went to bed. Shall I run up and look at him?'

'No,' said Paul's mother. 'No! Don't trouble yourself. It's all right. Don't sit up late. We shall be home fairly soon.'

'Very good,' said Miss Wilmot.

It was about one o'clock when Paul's mother and father drove up to their house. All was still. Paul's mother went to her room and slipped off her white fur coat. She heard her husband downstairs, preparing a drink.

And then, because of the strange anxiety in her heart, she went quietly upstairs to her son's room. She went softly along the upper passage. Was there a faint noise? What was it?

She stood outside his door, listening. There was a strange, heavy, but not loud noise. Her heart stood still. It was a soundless noise, but rushing and powerful. Something very large, moving violently. What was it? She ought to know. She felt that she knew the noise. She knew what it was.

But she could not be sure what it was. She couldn't say what it was. And on and on it went, like a madness. Softly, frozen with anxiety and fear, she turned the door handle.

The room was dark. But in the space near the window she heard and saw something moving backwards and forwards. She looked in fear and shock.

Then suddenly she turned on the light and saw her son madly riding the rocking horse. The bright light suddenly lit him up and shone on her as she stood in the doorway.

'Paul!' she cried. 'Whatever are you doing?'

'It's Malabar!' he shouted, in a strange, powerful voice. 'It's Malabar!'

His eyes burned at her for one senseless second as he stopped driving the wooden horse on. Then he fell with a crash to the ground and she, a mother's pain flooding over her, rushed to pick him up in her arms.

But he was unconscious, and unconscious he remained, with some kind of brain fever. He talked and moved restlessly, and his mother sat like a stone by his side.

'Malabar! It's Malabar! Bassett, Bassett, I *know*! It's Malabar!'

So the child cried, trying to get up and go to the rocking horse that gave him his ideas.

'What does he mean by Malabar?' asked the heart-frozen mother.

'I don't know,' said the father coldly.

'What does he mean by Malabar?' she asked her brother Oscar.

'It's one of the horses running for the Derby,' was the answer. And, in spite of himself, Oscar Creswell spoke to Bassett, and bet a thousand pounds on Malabar at fourteen to one.

The third day of the illness was very dangerous: they were waiting for a change. The boy, with his rather long, curly hair, was moving about all the time in bed. He neither slept nor became conscious again, and his eyes were like blue stones. His mother sat, feeling her heart had gone, actually turned into a stone.

In the evening Oscar Creswell did not come, but Bassett sent a message saying could he come up for one moment, just one moment? Paul's mother was very angry at first, but on second thoughts she agreed. The boy was the same as before. Perhaps Bassett might bring him to consciousness.

The gardener, a short man with sharp little brown eyes, came softly into the room and went to the bedside, looking at the restless, dying child.

'Master Paul!' he whispered. 'Master Paul! Malabar came in first all right, a good win. I did as you told me. You've made over seventy thousand pounds; you've got over eighty thousand. Malabar came first all right, Master Paul.'

'Malabar! Malabar! Did I say Malabar, Mother? Did I say Malabar? Do you think I'm lucky, Mother? I knew Malabar, didn't I? Over eighty thousand pounds! I call that lucky, don't you, Mother? Over eighty thousand pounds! I knew! Malabar came in all right. If I ride my horse until I'm sure, then I tell you, Bassett, you can bet as much as you like. Did you bet a lot, Bassett?'

'I bet a thousand on it, Master Paul.'

'I never told you, Mother, that if I can ride my horse, and *get there*, then I'm sure – oh, completely sure; Mother, did I ever tell you? I *am* lucky!'

'No, you never did,' said the mother.

But the boy died in the night.

And as he lay dead, his mother heard her brother's voice saying to her: 'Hester, you've got eighty thousand, and your son's dead. But, poor boy, poor boy, it's best for him to leave a life where he rides his rocking horse to find a winner.'

Springtime on the Menu   *O. Henry*

It was a day in March.

Never, never begin a story this way when you write one. No opening could possibly be worse. There is no imagination in it. It is flat and dry. But we can allow it here, because the following paragraph, which should have started the story, is too wild and impossible to be thrown in the face of the reader without preparation.

Sarah was crying over the menu.

To explain this you may guess that oysters were not listed, or that she had ordered onions, or that she had just come from the cinema. But all your guesses are wrong, and you will please let the story continue.

The gentleman who said that the world was an oyster which he would open with his sword became more famous than he deserved. It is not difficult to open an oyster with a sword. But did you ever notice anyone try to open it with a typewriter?

Sarah had managed to open the world a little with her typewriter. That was her work – typing. She did copy-typing and worked alone, not in an office.

The greatest success of Sarah's battle with the world was the arrangement that she made with Schulenberg's Home Restaurant. The restaurant was next door to the old redbrick building in which she had a room. One evening, after dining at Schulenberg's, Sarah took the menu away with her. It was written in almost unreadable handwriting, neither English nor German, and was so difficult to understand that if you were not careful you began with the sweet and ended with the soup and the day of the week.

The next day Sarah showed Schulenberg a beautifully

typewritten menu with the food listed in the right and proper places from the beginning to the words at the bottom: 'not responsible for coats and umbrellas.'

Schulenberg was very pleased. Before Sarah left him, he had made an agreement with her. She would provide typewritten menus for the 21 tables in the restaurant – a new one for each day's dinner, and new ones for breakfast and lunch as often as there were changes in the food or as neatness made necessary.

In return for this Schulenberg would send three meals a day to Sarah's room, and send her also each afternoon a list in pencil of the foods that were planned for Schulenberg's customers on the next day.

Both were satisfied with the agreement. Those who ate at Schulenberg's now knew what the food they were eating was called, even if its nature sometimes confused them. And Sarah had food during a cold, winter, which was the main thing for her.

When the spring months arrived, it was not spring. Spring comes when it comes. The frozen snows of January still lay hard outside. Men in the streets with their musical instruments still played "In the Good Old Summertime", with the expression and determination with which they had played it in December. The city was still in the power of winter.

One afternoon Sarah was shaking with cold in her bedroom. She had no work to do except Schulenberg's menus. Sarah sat in her rocking chair and looked out of the window. The month was a spring month and kept crying to her: 'Springtime is here, Sarah – springtime is here, I tell you. You've got a neat figure, Sarah – a nice, springtime figure – why do you look out of the window so sadly?'

Sarah's room was at the back of the house. Looking out of the window, she could see the windowless brick wall of the box factory in the next street. But she thought of grassy walks and trees and bushes and roses.

36

In the summer of last year Sarah had gone into the country and fallen in love with a farmer.

(In writing a story, never go backwards like this. It is bad art and destroys interest. Let it go forwards.)

Sarah stayed two weeks at Sunnybrook Farm. There she learned to love old Farmer Franklin's son, Walter. Farmers have been loved and married in less time. But young Walter Franklin was a modern farmer. He even had a telephone in the building where he milked the cows.

It was on a grassy walk that Walter had won her. And together they had sat and he had put dandelions in her hair. He had praised the effect of the yellow flowers against her brown hair; and she had left the flowers there, and walked back to the house swinging her hat in her hands.

They planned to marry in the spring – at the first signs of spring, Walter said. And Sarah came back to the city to hit the typewriter keys.

A knock at the door drove away Sarah's dreams of that happy day. A waiter had brought the rough pencil list of the Home Restaurant's next day's food written in old Schulenberg's pointed handwriting.

Sarah sat down at her typewriter and slipped a card beneath the rollers. She was a quick worker. Generally in an hour and a half the 21 cards were typed and ready.

Today there were more changes on the menu than usual. The soups were lighter; there were changes in the meat dishes. The spirit of spring filled the whole list.

Sarah's fingers danced over the typewriter like little flies above a summer stream. Down through the courses she worked, giving the name of each dish its proper position according to its length with a watchful eye.

Just above the sweets came the list of vegetables. And then–

Sarah was crying over the menu. Tears from the depths of

hopelessness rose in her heart and filled her eyes. Down went her head on the little typewriter stand.

For she had received no letter from Walter in two weeks, and the next thing on the menu was dandelions – dandelions with some kind of egg – but never mind the egg! – dandelions with whose golden flowers Walter had decorated the hair of his queen of love and future wife – dandelions, the messengers of spring – reminder of her happiest days.

But what a magical thing spring is! Into the great cold city of stone and iron a message had to be sent. There was none to bring it except the little messenger of the fields with his rough green coat, the dandelion – this lion's tooth, as the French call him. When he is in flower, he will help with lovemaking, twisted in my lady's nut-brown hair; when young, before he has his flowers, he goes into the boiling pot and delivers his message.

In a short time Sarah forced back her tears. The cards must be typed. But still in a faint, golden light from her dandelion dream, she fingered the typewriter keys absently for a little while, her mind and heart on the country walk with her young farmer. But soon she came back to the stone streets of Manhattan, and the typewriter began to jump.

At six o'clock the waiter brought her dinner and carried away the menus. While Sarah ate, she put the dish of dandelions sadly to one side. Just as a bright flower had been changed into a dark, unimportant vegetable, so her summer hopes had died.

At seven thirty the two people in the next room began to quarrel; the gas light went a little lower; someone started to unload coal; cats could be heard on the back fences. By these signs Sarah knew that it was time for her to read. She got out her book, settled her feet on her trunk, and began.

The front doorbell rang. The lady downstairs answered it. Sarah stopped reading and listened. Oh, yes; you would, just as she did!

And then a strong voice was heard in the hall below, and Sarah jumped for her door, leaving the book on the floor.

You have guessed it. She reached the top of the stairs just as her farmer came rushing up, and held her tightly in his arms.

'Why haven't you written – oh, why?' cried Sarah.

'New York is a rather large town,' said Walter Franklin. 'I came in, a week ago, to your old address. I found that you had gone away on a Thursday. The police and I have hunted for you ever since!'

'I wrote to you,' said Sarah, with feeling.

'Never got it!'

'Then how did you find me?'

The young farmer smiled a springtime smile.

'I went into the Home Restaurant next door this evening,' said he. 'I don't care who knows it; I like a dish of some kind of greens at this time of the year. I ran my eye down that nice typewritten menu looking for something like that. When I got to the vegetables, I knocked my chair over and shouted for the owner. He told me where you lived.'

'Why?'

'I'd know that capital W above the line that your typewriter makes anywhere in the world,' said Franklin.

The young man pulled a menu from his pocket, and pointed to a line.

Sarah recognized the first card she had typed that afternoon. There was still a mark in the upper right-hand corner where a tear had fallen. But over the spot where one should have read the name of a certain plant, the memory of their golden flowers had caused her fingers to strike strange keys.

Between two vegetables listed on the menu was the description:

Dearest ^Walter, with hard-boiled egg.

The Open Window   *H. H. Munro (Saki)*

'My aunt will come down very soon, Mr Nuttel,' said a calm and confident young lady of fifteen years of age. 'For now you must try to bear my company.'

Framton Nuttel tried to say the correct something which would please the girl in front of him, without causing unnecessary annoyance to the aunt that was still to come. He was supposed to be attempting a cure for his nerves, but he doubted whether these formal visits to a series of total strangers would help much.

'I know how it will be,' his sister had said, when he was preparing to move out into the country. 'You will bury yourself down there and not speak to a living soul, and your nerves will be worse than ever through loneliness. I shall just give you letters of introduction to all the people I know there. Some of them, as far as I can remember, were quite nice.'

Framton wondered whether Mrs Sappleton, the lady to whom he was bringing one of the letters of introduction, was one of the nice ones.

'Do you know many of the people round here?' asked the girl, when she thought that they had sat long enough in silence.

'Hardly any,' said Framton. 'My sister was staying here, you know, about four years ago, and she gave me letters of introduction to some of the people here.'

He made the last statement with obvious sadness.

'Then you know almost nothing about my aunt?' continued the confident young lady.

'Only her name and address,' Framton admitted. He was wondering whether Mrs Sappleton was still married, or whether her husband had died. But there was something about the room that suggested a man's presence.

'Her great sorrow came just three years ago,' said the child.

'Her sorrow?' asked Framton. Somehow, in this restful country place, sorrows seemed out of place.

'You may wonder why we keep that window wide open on an October afternoon,' said the girl, pointing to a large French window* that opened onto the grass outside.

'It is quite warm for the time of the year,' said Framton; 'but has that window got anything to do with your aunt's sorrow?'

'Out through that window, exactly three years ago, her husband and her two young brothers went off for their day's shooting. They never came back. While they were walking across to the shooting ground, they were all three swallowed up in a bog. It had been that terrible wet summer, you know, and places that were safe in other years became suddenly dangerous. Their bodies were never found. That was the worst part of it.' Here the child's voice lost its confidence and became unsteadily human. 'Poor aunt always thinks that they will come back some day, they and the little brown dog that was lost with them, and walk in through that window just as they used to do. That is why the window is kept open every evening until it is quite dark. Poor dear aunt, she has often told me how they went out, her husband with his white coat over his arm, and Ronnie, her youngest brother, singing a song, as he always did to annoy her because she said it upset her. Do you know, sometimes on still, quiet evenings like this, I almost get a strange feeling that they will all walk in through that window...'

She stopped and trembled. It was a relief to Framton when the aunt came busily into the room and said how sorry she was for her late appearance.

'I hope Vera has been amusing you?' she said.

*French window: a door made of glass, usually opening out on to the garden.

'She has been very interesting,' said Framton.

'I hope you don't mind the window open,' said Mrs Sappleton brightly. 'My husband and brothers will be home soon from shooting, and they always come in this way. They've been shooting birds today near the bog, so they'll make my poor floors dirty. So typical of you men, isn't it?'

She talked on cheerfully about the shooting and the lack of birds, and the hope of shooting duck in the winter. To Framton it was all quite terrible. He made a great effort, which was only partly successful, to turn the talk to a more pleasant subject. He was conscious that his hostess was giving him only a part of her attention, and her eyes were frequently looking past him to the open window and the grass beyond. It was certainly unfortunate that he should have paid his visit on this sad day.

'The doctors agree in ordering me complete rest, no mental excitement and no violent physical exercise,' announced Framton, who had the usual mistaken idea that total strangers want to know every detail of one's illnesses, their cause and cure. 'On the matter of food, they are not so much in agreement,' he continued.

'No?' said Mrs Sappleton, sounding tired and even perhaps a little bored. Then she suddenly brightened into attention – but not to what Framton was saying.

'Here they are at last!' she cried. 'Just in time for tea, and don't they look as if they were muddy up to the eyes!'

Framton trembled slightly and turned towards the girl with a look intended to show sympathetic understanding. The child was looking out through the open window with fear in her eyes. With a shock Framton turned round in his seat and looked in the same direction.

In the deepening darkness three figures were walking across the grass towards the house; they all carried guns under their arms, and one of them also had a white coat hanging over his shoulders. A tired brown dog kept close to their heels. Noiselessly they neared the house, and then a young voice started to sing in the darkness.

Framton seized his hat and stick; he ran out through the hall door, up the drive and through the front gate. He almost ran into a man on a bicycle.

'Here we are, my dear,' said the bearer of the white coat, coming in through the window; 'fairly muddy, but most of it's dry. Who was that who ran out as we came up?'

'A very strange man, a Mr Nuttel,' said Mrs Sappleton. 'He could only talk about his illnesses, and ran off without a word of excuse or goodbye when you arrived. It was as if he had seen a ghost.'

'I expect it was the dog,' said the girl calmly; 'he told me he had a terrible fear of dogs. He was once hunted into a graveyard somewhere in India by a pack of wild dogs, and had to spend the night in a newly dug grave with the creatures standing over him. Enough to make anyone lose their nerve.'

She was very quick and clever with her imagination.

The Income-Tax Man *Mark Twain*

The first notice that was taken of me when I 'settled down' recently, was by a gentleman who said he was an assessor, a word that I did not understand very well. I said I had never heard of his branch of business before, but I was very glad to see him in spite of that – would he sit down? He sat down. I did not have anything particular to say, but I felt that people who have arrived at the important position of keeping a house must be conversational, must be easy and friendly in society. So, as I could think of nothing else to say, I asked him if he was opening his shop in our neighbourhood.

He said he was. (I did not wish to appear to know nothing, but I *had* hoped he would mention what he had for sale.)

'How is trade?' I asked him. And he said, 'Fair.'

I then said we would visit his shop, and if we liked it as well as any other, we would give him our business.

He said he thought we would like his place of business well enough to use no other – he said he had never met anybody who would go off and hunt up another man in the same kind of business after trading with him once.

That sounded rather too confident; but the man looked honest enough.

I do not know how it happened exactly, but gradually we appeared to become more friendly in our conversation, and then everything went along very comfortably.

We talked and talked and talked – at least I did; and we laughed and laughed and laughed – at least he did. But all the time my mind was working hard. I was determined to find out all about his business in spite of his mysterious answers – and I was determined that I would get it out of him without him knowing what I was doing. I intended to trap him with a deep, deep trick. I would tell him all about my own business; and he would naturally grow to like me so much that he would forget to be careful, and he would tell me all about *his* affairs before he realized what I was trying to do.

I thought of saying to him, 'Sir, you little know what a clever person you are dealing with.' But I said:

'Now you would never guess how much money I made giving talks to people this winter and last spring.'

'No – I don't believe I could, to save my life. Let me see – let me see. About two thousand dollars, perhaps? But no; no, sir, I know you couldn't have made so much as that. Say seventeen hundred?'

'Ha! ha! I knew you couldn't guess. I received for my talks last spring and this winter fourteen thousand seven hundred and fifty dollars. What do you think of that?'

'Well, it's very surprising – that's a very large amount of money. I will make a note of it. And you say even this wasn't all?'

'All! My dear sir, there was my income from the newspaper – the Daily Warwhoop – for four months – about – about – well, what would you say to about eight thousand dollars, for example?'

'Say! Well, I should say I should like to see myself rolling in just such an ocean of money. Eight thousand! I'll make a note of it. Well, man! And in addition to all this, am I to understand that you had still more income?'

'Ha! ha! ha! You're only at the beginning of it. I wrote a book – *The Innocents Abroad* – price three and a half to five dollars, according to the cover. Listen to me. Look me in the eye. During the last four months and a half, not to mention sales before that, but just simply during the four months and a half, we've sold ninety-five thousand copies of that book. Ninety-five thousand! Think of it. Average four dollars a copy, perhaps. It's nearly four hundred thousand dollars, my dear sir. I get half.'

'Good heavens! I'll write that down. Fourteen-seven-fifty –
eight – two hundred. Total, about – well, I can hardly believe it –
the total is about two hundred and thirteen or fourteen thousand
dollars! *Is* that possible?'

'Possible! If there's any mistake, it's the other way. It's more.
Two hundred and fourteen thousand is my income for this year,
if I know how to add up.'

Then the gentleman got up to go. I thought with discomfort
that perhaps I had told all these secrets for nothing, besides being
persuaded to make them a lot greater because of the stranger's
surprised cries. But no; at the last moment the gentleman handed
me a large envelope, and said that it contained everything I might
like to know about his business; and that he would be happy to
have my business – would in fact be proud to have the business of
a man with such a large income; and that he used to think there
were a number of rich men in the city, but when they came to
trade with him, he discovered that they hardly had enough to live
on; and that, in truth, it had been such a long, long time since he
had seen a rich man face to face, and talked with him, and
touched him with his hands, that he could hardly stop himself
from throwing his arms round me – in fact, he would be very
grateful if I would *let* him throw his arms round me.

This so pleased me that I did not try to stop him, but allowed
this simple-hearted stranger to throw his arms around me. And
then he went on his way.

As soon as he had gone, I opened his envelope. I studied the
papers carefully for four minutes. I then called the cook, and said:

'Hold me while I faint.'

Ah, what an evil man he was! His envelope contained nothing
in the world except a form on which to record my income for
the purpose of income tax – a long list of impolite questions
about my private affairs, filling the best part of four long pages of

small print – questions, I may say, formed with such wonderful skill that the oldest and wisest man in the world couldn't understand the meaning of most of them – questions, too, that were designed to make a man report about four times his actual income to stop himself telling a lie. I looked for a way out of my troubles, but there did not appear to be any. Inquiry Number 1 covered my case generously and completely:

What were your profits, during the past year, from any trade, business, or work, wherever carried on?

And that inquiry was followed by 13 others of an equally searching nature. The gentlest of them demanded information about whether I had been a robber on the open road, or whether I had set fire to anything, or had any other secret way of getting money, or had received any property which was not mentioned in my statement of income as stated opposite Inquiry Number 1.

It was very clear that the stranger had let me make a fool of myself. By encouraging my pride, the stranger had persuaded me to admit to an income of two hundred and fourteen thousand dollars. It appeared that by law one thousand of this was free from income tax – which was only a drop in the ocean. At the legal rate of five per cent, I had to pay over to the Government in tax the terrible sum of ten thousand six hundred and fifty dollars!

(I should say, at this stage, that I did not do it.)

I know a very wealthy man whose house is a palace, whose table is kingly, who spends a great deal, but a man who has no income, as I have often noticed when looking at the list of taxes paid by other citizens. And to him I went for advice.

He took my papers, he put on his glasses, he picked up his pen, and suddenly – I was a very poor man. It was the neatest thing that ever was. He did it simply by cleverly arranging the list of allowances.

He wrote down my "state, national and city taxes" as so much; my "losses by flood, fire and so on" as so much; my "losses on sales of property", and "animals sold", on "payments for rent of home", on "repairs and improvements" as so much. He wrote down "salary, already taxed, as an officer of the United States army or other service" as so much. He wrote down other things. He found unbelievable amounts to set against my income from each one of these allowances – each and every one of them. And when he had finished, he handed me the paper, and I saw immediately that during the year my income, as profits, had been *one thousand two hundred and fifty dollars and forty cents.*

'Now,' he said, 'the thousand dollars is free from tax by law. What you must do is to go and swear that this information is true and then pay tax on the two hundred and fifty dollars.'

(While he was making this speech, his little boy Willie lifted a two-dollar note out of his pocket and disappeared with it, and I feel quite sure that if my stranger went to see that little boy tomorrow, the boy would tell lies about his income.)

'Do you,' said I, 'do you always arrange the allowances in this way for your own income, sir?'

'Well, of course. If we didn't have those 11 questions under the heading of allowances, I would become a beggar every year in order to support this hateful and evil, this cruel and terrible government.'

This gentleman stands very high among the very best of the rich men of the city – the men of moral value, of high business standards, of great social standing – and so I accepted his suggestion. I went down to the tax office, and under the cold eyes of my previous visitor I stood up and swore to lie after lie, trick after trick, until my soul was coated with a thick layer of lies and my self-respect was gone for ever.

The Upper Berth *F. Marion Crawford*

We had talked for a long time, and the conversation was beginning to fail; the tobacco smoke had got into the heavy curtains, the wine had got into our brains, and it was already perfectly clear that the meeting might soon come to its natural end, and we, the guests, would go home to bed and most certainly to sleep. No one had said anything very interesting; it may be that no one had anything very interesting to say.

It was then that Brisbane spoke, and we all looked at him. He was a man of about thirty-five, and had those gifts which chiefly attract the attention of men. He was a strong man. There was nothing unusual about his appearance, though his size was above the average. He was almost 2 metres in height; he did not appear to be fat, but on the other hand he was certainly not thin. His small head was supported by a strong neck, and he had powerful hands and an unusually thick chest. He was one of those men who look extremely strong and are really much stronger than they look.

'It is a very strange thing,' said Brisbane.

Everybody stopped talking. Brisbane's voice was not loud, but it had a sharp quality which could cut through general conversation like a knife. Everybody listened. Brisbane noticed that he had attracted their attention.

'It is a very strange thing,' he continued, 'about ghosts. People are always asking whether anybody has seen a ghost. I have.'

'Nonsense! What, you? You don't mean to say so, Brisbane!'

Cries from all sides greeted Brisbane's surprising statement. The situation was saved. Brisbane was going to tell a story.

◆

49

I am an old sailor, said Brisbane, and as I have to cross the Atlantic fairly often, there are ships that I particularly like. I have a habit of waiting for certain ships when it is necessary for me to sail. I have always had good crossings, with one exception.

I remember it very well; it was a warm morning in June. I did not have much luggage – I never have. The *Kamtschatka* was one of the ships I liked best. I say was, because she certainly no longer is. I cannot think of anything in the world which would make me travel on her again. Yes, I know what you are going to say: she's a good ship; she has a lot of advantages. But I won't cross in her again. Well, I got on board and called a steward whose red nose I remembered.

'One hundred and five, lower berth,' said I, in the voice of those men who cross the Atlantic frequently and think nothing of it.

The steward took my bag and my coat. I shall never forget the expression on his face. He did not, in fact, turn pale; but from his expression I judged that he was either about to cry bitter tears, or to drop my bag. As the bag contained two bottles of particularly fine wine, given to me by my old friend Snigginson van Pickyns, I felt extremely nervous. But the steward neither dropped a tear nor dropped the bag.

He gave a low cry of surprise, and led the way. I supposed that he had had something to drink, but I said nothing and followed him down into the lower parts of the ship. Number 105 was rather towards the back of the ship; there was nothing noticeable about the room. The lower berth, like most of those on the *Kamtschatka*, was double. There was plenty of space; there was the usual washing place and, above the sink, glass bottles filled with unpleasant-smelling brown liquid.

The steward put down my bag and looked at me as if he wanted to get away – probably in search of more passengers and more coins. It is always a good idea to make friends with these men, and so I gave him a few coins there and then.

'I'll try and make you as comfortable as I can,' he said as he put the coins in his pocket. But in his voice there was a note of doubt which surprised me. Perhaps the money I had given him was not enough, and he was not satisfied; I thought that he was probably slightly drunk. But I was wrong, and unfair to the man.

◆

Nothing really worth mentioning happened during that day. We left on time and it was very pleasant to be on our way, because the weather was warm and the movement of the ship brought us some air. Everybody knows what the first day at sea is like. People walk about and look at each other, and sometimes meet friends whom they did not know were on board. There is the usual uncertainty as to whether the food will be good or bad until the first two meals have put the matter beyond doubt. There is the usual uncertainty about the weather. The tables are crowded at first; but then pale-faced people jump up from their seats and rush towards the door, and each old sailor breathes more freely as his seasick neighbour runs away and leaves him with more room and more food.

One crossing of the Atlantic is very much like another, and we who cross it often do not make the journey for its interest. To most of us the most pleasant moment of the day is when we have taken our last walk in the open air, have had our last smoke and, having succeeded in tiring ourselves, feel free to go to bed unashamed.

On that first night I felt particularly lazy, and I went to bed in 105 rather earlier than I usually do. As I arrived, I was surprised to see that I was going to have a companion. A bag, very like my own, lay in the opposite corner, and there was a stick on the upper berth. I had hoped to be alone, and I was disappointed; but I wondered who my companion was.

51

Before I had been in bed long, he entered. He was, as far as I could see, a very tall man, very thin, very pale, with sandy hair and grey eyes. He was the sort of man you might see in Wall Street or at the Café Anglais, who always seems to be alone; you might meet him at the races, but he would never appear to be doing anything there either. A little overdressed – a little strange. There are three or four of his kind on every ocean ship. I made up my mind that I did not want to know him, and I went to sleep saying to myself that I would study his habits in order to avoid him. If he rose early, I would rise later; if he went to bed late, I would go to bed early. I did not wish to know him. Poor man! I need not have taken the trouble to make so many decisions about him, since I never saw him again after that first night in 105.

I was sleeping deeply when I was suddenly woken by a loud noise. To judge from the sound, my companion must have jumped down from the upper berth to the floor in a single movement. I heard him trying to open the door; it opened, and then I heard his footsteps as he ran at full speed down the passage, leaving the door open behind him. The ship was rolling a little, and I expected to hear him fall, but he ran as though he were running for his life. The door continued to swing open and shut with the movement of the ship, and the sound annoyed me. I got up and closed it, and found my way back to my berth in the darkness. I went to sleep again; but I have no idea how long I slept.

When I awoke it was still dark, but I felt unpleasantly cold, and it seemed to me that there was a dampness in the air. You know the strange smell of a place that has been flooded with sea water. I covered myself up as well as I could and went to sleep again, thinking of complaints to be made the next day, and choosing the most powerful words in the language. I could hear my companion turn over in the upper berth. He had probably returned while I was asleep. Once I thought he cried out in pain, and I told myself that he was seasick. That is particularly unpleasant when one is below. But I slept until early daylight.

The ship was rolling heavily, much more than on the evening before, and the light which came in through the small round window changed in colour with every movement according to whether the side of the ship was facing the sea or the sky. It was very cold – especially for the month of June. I turned my head and looked at the window, and saw to my surprise that it was wide open and held back with a hook. I was very angry. Then I got up and shut it. As I turned back, I looked at the upper berth. The curtains around it were pulled close together; my companion had probably felt as cold as I had. I thought I had slept enough. The room was uncomfortable – though, strange to say, I could not smell the dampness which had annoyed me in the night. My companion was still asleep – an excellent opportunity for avoiding him – so I dressed immediately and went outside. The day was warm and cloudy, with an oily swell on the water.

It was seven o'clock as I came out – much later than I had imagined. I met the doctor, who was taking his first breath of morning air. He was a young man from the west of Ireland – a large man, with black hair and blue eyes, already rather fat; he had a happy, healthy look which was rather attractive.

'Fine morning,' I said, by way of introduction.

'Well,' he said, looking at me with an appearance of friendly interest, 'it's a fine morning and it's not a fine morning. I don't think it's much of a morning.'

'Well, no – it is not so very fine,' said I. 'It was cold last night, I thought. But when I looked around, I found that the window was wide open. I had not noticed it when I went to bed. And my room was damp too.'

'Damp!' said he. 'Where is it?'

'One hundred and five.'

To my surprise the doctor reacted by giving me a quick, strange look.

'What is the matter?' I asked.

'Oh – nothing,' he answered; 'but everybody has complained of that room for the last three trips.'

'I shall complain too,' I said. 'It's damp.'

'I don't believe it can be helped,' answered the doctor. 'I believe there is something – well, it is not my business to frighten passengers.'

'You need not be afraid of frightening me,' I replied. 'I can bear any amount of damp. If I get a bad cold, I will come to you immediately.'

'It is not so much the dampness,' he said. 'But I expect you will get on very well. Have you anyone with you there?'

'Yes; a terrible man, who goes out in the middle of the night, and leaves the door open.'

Again the doctor looked at me closely. But he looked serious.

'Did he come back?' he asked.

'Yes. I was asleep, but I woke up, and heard him moving. Then I felt cold and went to sleep again. This morning I found the window open.'

'Listen,' said the doctor quietly. 'I don't much like this ship, but I have a good-sized room which I will share with you, though I don't know who you are.'

I was very much surprised at the suggestion. I could not imagine why he should take such a sudden interest in me. But his manner, as he spoke of the ship, was strange.

'You are very good, Doctor,' I said. 'But really I believe even now that the room could be cleaned out. Why do you not like the ship?'

'We do not believe in unnatural events in our profession, sir,' he said, 'but the sea makes people do that. I don't want to frighten you, but if you will take my advice, you will move in here. I would rather see you in the sea than know that you or any other man were sleeping in 105.'

'Good heavens! Why?' I asked.

'Just because on the last three trips all the people who have slept there actually *have* gone into the sea,' he answered.

The news was surprising and extremely unpleasant, I admit. I looked hard at the doctor to see whether he was joking, but he seemed perfectly serious. I thanked him warmly for his offer, but I told him that I was going to be the one man who slept in that particular room and did not fall into the sea. He did not say much, but looked as serious as ever, and he seemed to think that before we reached the other side of the Atlantic I would change my mind.

We went to breakfast, but not many passengers were there. I noticed that one or two officers who breakfasted with us looked very serious. After the meal I went to my room to get a book. The curtains of the upper berth were still tightly closed. Not a word was to be heard. My companion was probably still asleep.

As I came out, I met the steward whose business it was to look after me. He whispered that the captain wanted to see me, and then he ran off down the passage as if he was very anxious to avoid any questions. I found the captain waiting for me.

'Sir,' he said, 'I want to ask if you would do something for me.'

I answered that I would do anything he wished.

'The man who slept in your room,' he said, 'has disappeared. He is known to have gone to bed early last night. Did you notice anything strange in his manner?'

The question, coming after the doctor's words half an hour earlier, shocked me greatly.

'You don't mean to say that he has fallen into the sea?' I asked.

'I fear he has,' answered the captain.

'This is most strange . . .' I began.

'Why?' he asked.

'He is the fourth,' I explained. In answer to another question from the captain I said, without mentioning the doctor, that I had heard the story concerning 105. He seemed very much annoyed at hearing that I knew of it. I told him what had happened in the night.

'What you say,' he replied, 'is almost exactly the same as what was told me by the companions of two of the other three. They jump out of bed and run down the passage. Two of them were seen to fall into the sea; we stopped and lowered boats, but they were not found. But nobody saw or heard the man who was lost last night – if he really is lost. The steward, who perhaps expected something to go wrong, went to look for him this morning and found his berth empty. His clothes were lying about, just as he had left them. The steward was the only man on board who knew him by sight, and he has been looking everywhere for him. He has disappeared! Now, sir, I want to beg you not to mention this to any of the passengers; I don't want the ship to get a bad name. You can choose any one of the officers' rooms you like, including my own, for the rest of the journey. Is that fair?'

'Very,' said I; 'and I thank you very much. But now I have that room to myself and am alone there; so I would rather not move. If the steward will take out that unfortunate man's things, I would like to stay where I am. I will not say anything about the matter, and I think I can promise you that I will not follow my companion.'

The captain argued with me; but I preferred to be alone in my room. If I moved, I would have to share a room with an officer. I do not know whether I acted foolishly, but if I had taken his advice, I would have nothing more to tell.

But that was not the end of the matter. I made up my mind that I would not be upset by such stories. I told the captain that there was something wrong with the room. It was rather damp. The window had been left open last night. Perhaps my companion was ill when he came on board, and perhaps he became feverish after he went to bed. He might even now be hiding somewhere on board, and might be found later. The room ought to be cleaned, and the lock on the window ought to be mended. I asked the captain's permission to have these things done.

'Of course you have a right to stay where you are if you please,' he replied; 'but I wish you would move somewhere else, and let me lock the place up.'

I could not agree, and I went away after promising to be silent concerning the man's disappearance. He was not missed during the course of the day. Towards evening I met the doctor again, and he asked me whether I had changed my mind. I told him I had not.

'You soon will,' he said, very seriously.

◆

We played cards in the evening, and I went to bed late. I will admit now that I had an unpleasant feeling when I entered my room. I could not help thinking of the tall man I had seen the night before, who was now drowned and dead. His face appeared clearly in front of me as I undressed. I locked the door. Suddenly I noticed that the window was open, and hooked back. This was more than I could bear. I went out in search of Robert, my steward. I was very angry, I remember, and when I found him I dragged him roughly to the door of 105, and pushed him towards the open window.

'What do you mean by leaving that window open every night? Don't you know that it's against the rules? Don't you know that if the ship rolled and the water began to come in, ten men could not shut it? I will report you to the captain for placing the ship in danger!'

I was extremely angry. The man trembled and turned pale,

and then began to shut the round window with the heavy metal screw.

'Why don't you answer me?' I demanded.

'If you please, sir,' said Robert, 'there's nobody on board that can keep this window shut at night. You can try it yourself, sir. I'm not going to stay on board this ship any longer, sir. But if I was you, sir, I'd go and sleep somewhere else: with the doctor, sir. Look, sir. Is that shut safely, do you think, sir? Try it, sir, and see if it will move.'

I tried the window and found it perfectly tight.

'Well, sir,' continued Robert, 'in half an hour it will be open again; and hooked back, too, sir; that's the terrible thing – hooked back!'

I examined the great screw.

'If I find it open in the night, Robert, I will give you a pound. It is not possible. You may go.'

'A pound, did you say, sir? Very good, sir. Thank you, sir. Good night, sir. A pleasant rest and all manner of lovely dreams, sir!'

Robert hurried away, glad to go. Of course I did not believe him. The result was that he got his money, and I spent a strangely unpleasant night.

I went to bed, and five minutes afterwards Robert put out the light that burned steadily in the passage, the other side of the door. I lay quite still in the dark trying to go to sleep, but I soon found that impossible. I was no longer sleepy, and I lay awake for some time, sometimes looking at the window, which I could just see from where I lay. I believe I must have lain there for an hour; and, as I remember, I was just going off into sleep when I was woken by a current of cold air. I also felt some drops of salt water blown on my face. I jumped up; but the movement of the ship threw me violently across the room. I got back onto my knees. The window was again wide open and hooked back!

Now these things are facts. I was wide awake when I got up,

and I should certainly have been woken by the fall if I had been asleep. There were marks on my body on the following morning to prove that I had fallen. The window was wide open and hooked back: a thing so difficult to explain that I remember very well feeling shock rather than fear when I discovered it. I immediately closed it again and turned the screw with all my strength. It was very dark in the room.

I decided to watch the window to see whether it would open again. The metal screw was very heavy and not at all easy to turn; I could not believe that it had been turned by the shaking of the ship's engines. I stood there looking out at the sea; I must have remained there for a quarter of an hour.

Suddenly, as I stood, I heard something moving behind me in one of the berths, and a moment afterwards I heard a faint cry of pain. I ran across the room and pulled the curtains of the upper berth apart, pushing my hands in to discover if there was anyone there. There was someone.

I remember that the feeling as I put my hands forward was as though I were pushing them into damp air; and from behind the curtains came a wind that smelled strongly of seawater. I got hold of something that had the shape of a man's arm, but was smooth, and wet, and icy cold. But suddenly, as I pulled, the creature moved violently forward against me, heavy and wet, but unnaturally strong. I fell back; and in a moment the door opened and the thing rushed out. I had not had time to be frightened, and I ran through the door and followed at top speed. But I was too late. Nine metres in front of me I could see – I am sure I saw it – a dark shadow moving along the badly lighted passage. But in a moment it had disappeared. I shook from head to toe. I am not ashamed of it at all: I was badly frightened.

Still I doubted my senses: perhaps it was a bad dream caused by something I had eaten. I went back to the room and entered it with an effort. The whole place smelled of seawater, as it had when I had woken the evening before. I lit a lamp and saw that the window was open again, and a terrible fear came over me which I had never felt before nor wish to feel again. I examined the upper berth and expected to find it damp with seawater.

But I was disappointed. The bed had been slept in, and the smell of the sea was strong; but the bedclothes were as dry as a bone. I thought perhaps that Robert had not had the courage to make the bed after the accident the night before – it had all just been a very bad dream. I pulled the curtains back as far as I could and examined the place carefully. It was perfectly dry. But the window was open again. In a state of confusion, I closed it and screwed it down: I used a heavy stick to turn the screw and pressed with all my strength until the thick metal began to bend under the force. Then I sat down. I sat there all night, unable to think of rest – hardly able to think at all. But the window remained closed, and I did not believe it would now open again without the use of great force.

The morning came at last, and I dressed myself slowly, thinking over all that had happened in the night. It was a beautiful day, and I went outside, glad to get into the early, pure sunshine, and to smell the air from the blue water, so different from the air in that room. I saw the doctor, with a pipe in his mouth, enjoying the air just as on the day before.

'Good morning,' he said, looking at me with interest.

'Doctor, you were quite right,' said I. 'There is something wrong with that place.'

'I thought you would change your mind,' he answered. 'You've had a bad night, I suppose. Shall I give you a drink?'

'No, thanks,' I cried. 'But I would like to tell you what happened.'

I then tried to explain as clearly as possible what had taken place, and I added that I had been frightened as never in my life before. I mentioned the window particularly; that was a fact, even if the rest had been a dream. I had closed it twice in the night.

'You seem to think I may doubt the story,' said the doctor, smiling at the detailed account of the state of the window. 'I do not doubt it in the least. I invite you again. Bring your luggage here and share my room with me.'

'Come and share mine for one night,' I said. 'Help me to solve this mystery.'

'If you stay there, you'll end up in the sea,' said he.

'Do you really believe it is a ghost?' I inquired with a laugh. But as I spoke, I remembered very well the feelings that had filled me in the night. The doctor turned sharply on me.

'Have you any reasonable explanation of these things to offer?' he asked. 'No, you have not. Well, you say you will find an explanation. I say that you won't, sir, simply because there is none.'

'But, my dear sir,' I replied, 'do you, as a man of science, mean to tell me that such things cannot be explained?'

'I do,' he answered. 'And if they could, I would not be interested in the explanation.'

I did not wish to spend another night alone in that place, but I was determined to find the cause of the strange events. I do not believe there are many men who would have slept there alone, after passing two such nights. But I decided to try it if I could not get anyone to share with me. The doctor did not want to join me, and he informed me that there was no one on board who would be likely to join me.

A little later I met the captain and told him my story.

'Listen,' he said. 'I will tell you what I will do. I will share your watch myself, and we will see what happens. It is my belief that we can solve this mystery together. There may be someone hiding on board, who travels free by frightening the passengers.'

I was very pleased by the captain's offer to spend the night with me. He sent for a workman and ordered him to do anything

I wanted. We went below immediately. I had all the bedclothes taken out of the upper berth, and we examined the place thoroughly to see if there was a board loose anywhere, or part of the wall which could be opened or pushed apart. We examined the floor and took the lower berth to pieces. In fact there was no part of the room which was not searched and tested. Everything was in perfect order and we put everything back in its place. As we were finishing our work, Robert came to the door and looked in.

'Well, sir – find anything, sir?' he asked.

'You were right about the window, Robert,' I said, and I gave him the promised money. Then the workman spoke.

'It's my belief, sir,' he said, 'that you'd better move, and let me lock the room up by putting some long screws through the door. Four lives have been lost out of here, and in four trips. Better give it up, sir – better give it up!'

'I will try it for one more night,' I said.

My spirits had risen at the thought of having the captain's company, and I made up my mind not to be prevented from getting to the bottom of the strange business.

◆

The captain was one of those cheerful sailors whose courage and calmness in times of difficulty lead them naturally to high positions of trust. He was not the man to be discouraged by a silly story.

At about ten o'clock that evening, as I was having a last smoke, he came up to me and took me to one side.

'This is a serious matter, Mr Brisbane,' he said. 'We shall either be disappointed, or have a rough time. I cannot laugh at the affair, and I will ask you to sign your name to a statement of whatever happens. If nothing happens tonight, we will try again tomorrow and the next day. Are you ready?'

So we went below and entered the room. Robert watched us as we went in as though he were certain that something terrible was about to happen. The captain closed the door behind us and locked it.

'Let us put your bag in front of the door,' he suggested. 'One of us can sit on it. Nothing can get out then. Is the window screwed down?'

I found it as I had left it in the morning. In fact, without using some kind of metal bar or heavy stick, as I had done, no one could have opened it. I pulled back the curtains of the upper berth so that I could see well into it. The captain sat on the bag, and asked me to search the room thoroughly. This was soon done.

'It is impossible for any human being to get in,' I said, 'or for any human being to open the window.'

'Very good,' said the captain calmly. 'If we see anything now, it must be either imagination or something inhuman and unnatural.'

I sat down on the edge of the lower berth.

'The first time it happened,' said the captain, 'was in March. The passenger who slept here, in the upper berth, turned out to be a madman. He rushed out in the middle of the night and threw himself into the sea before anyone could stop him.'

'I suppose that often happens,' I said.

'Not often – no. Never before in my experience, though I have heard of it happening on board other ships. On the very next trip– What are you looking at?' he asked suddenly.

I believe I gave no answer. My eyes were fixed on the window. It seemed to me that the metal screw was beginning to turn very slowly – so slowly that I was not sure it moved at all. Seeing where I was looking, the captain looked too.

'It's moving!' he whispered. 'No, it isn't,' he added after a minute.

I rose and tried it. It was certainly loosened; with an effort I could move it with my hands.

'The strange thing,' said the captain, 'is that the second man who was lost is supposed to have got out through that same window. It was in the middle of the night, and the weather was very heavy. It was said that one of the windows was open and the sea was running in. I came below and found everything flooded and the window wide open. Well, we managed to shut it, but the water did some damage. Ever since then, the room has smelt of sea water from time to time. We supposed the passenger had thrown himself out, but I don't see how he did it. I can smell it now, can't you?' he asked.

'Yes,' I said. 'The place must be damp; but when we examined it this morning, everything was perfectly dry. It is most strange. Oh!'

The lamp went out. There was still a good deal of light from a lamp in the passage outside. The ship rolled heavily, and the curtain of the upper berth swung far out into the room and back again.

At the same moment the captain jumped to his feet with a loud cry of surprise; I turned and hurried towards him. He was using all his strength on the screw of the window. It seemed to turn against his hands in spite of all his efforts. I quickly picked up the heavy stick that I always used to carry, put it through the ring and pressed down with all my strength. But the strong wood broke suddenly and I fell down. When I rose again, the window was wide open, and the captain was standing with his back against the door, pale to the lips.

'There is something in that berth!' he cried in a strange voice, his eyes almost jumping out of his head. 'Hold the door while I look – it will not escape us, whatever it is!'

But instead of taking his place, I jumped onto the lower berth and reaching up, seized something which lay in the upper berth.

It was something ghostly, terrible beyond words, and it moved

64

in my hands. It was like the body of a man long drowned, but it moved and had the strength of ten living men. I held it with all my force – the slippery, wet, terrible thing. The dead white eyes seemed to look at me out of the darkness; the smell of seawater was all around it, and the shiny hair hung in wet curls over its dead face. I fought with the thing; it forced me back and nearly broke my arms. It threw its arms around my neck. Finally I fell.

It jumped across me and seemed to throw itself on the captain. When I last saw him on his feet, his face was white and his lips pressed tightly together. It seemed to me that he struck the thing violently, and then he, too, fell forward on his face with a cry.

The thing paused for a moment; but I could not cry out, because I had no voice left. The thing disappeared suddenly and it seemed to me that it went out through the open window; but how that was possible, through such a small opening, is more than anyone can tell. I lay on the floor for a long time, and the captain lay beside me. At last I moved, and I knew immediately that my left arm was broken.

I got to my feet, and with my remaining hand I tried to raise the captain. At last he moved; he was not hurt, but he seemed hardly conscious.

◆

Well, do you want to hear any more? There is nothing more. That is the end of my story. Long screws were put through the door of 105; and if ever you want to travel in that room, you will be told that it is not free.

I finished the trip in the doctor's room. He took care of my broken arm and told me not to play with ghosts again. The captain was very silent, and never sailed in that ship again, though she is still running. And I will not sail in her either. It was a very unpleasant experience, and I was very badly frightened. That is all. That is how I saw a ghost – if it was a ghost.

My Bank Account   *Stephen Leacock*

When I go into a bank I get frightened. The clerks frighten me; the desks frighten me; the sight of the money frightens me; everything frightens me. The moment I pass through the doors of a bank and attempt to do business there, I become an irresponsible fool.

I knew this before, but my salary had been raised to fifty dollars a month and I felt that the bank was the only place for it.

So I walked unsteadily in and looked round at the clerks with fear. I had an idea that a person who was about to open an account must necessarily speak to the manager.

I went up to a desk marked "Accountant". The accountant was a tall, confident devil. The very sight of him frightened me. My voice sounded as if it came from the grave.

'Can I see the manager?' I said, and added, 'Alone.' I don't know why I said 'alone'.

'Certainly,' said the accountant, and brought him.

The manager was a calm, serious man. I held my fifty-six dollars, pressed together in a ball, in my pocket.

'Are you the manager?' I said. God knows, I didn't doubt it.

'Yes,' he said.

'Can I see you,' I asked, 'alone?' I didn't want to say 'alone' again, but without this word the question seemed senseless.

The manager looked at me with some anxiety. He felt that I had a terrible secret to tell.

'Come in here,' he said, and led the way to a private room. He turned the key in the lock.

'We are safe from interruption here,' he said. 'Sit down.'

We both sat down and looked at each other. I was speechless. I did not know what to say next.

'You are one of Pinkerton's★ detectives, I suppose,' he said.

My mysterious manner had made him think that I was a detective. I knew what he was thinking, and it made me worse.

'No, not from Pinkerton's,' I said, seeming to mean that I was a detective but was not from Pinkerton's.

'To tell the truth,' I went on, as if someone had urged me to tell lies about it, 'I am not a detective at all. I have come to open an account. I intend to keep all my money in this bank.'

The manager looked relieved but still serious; he felt sure now that I was a very rich man, perhaps a member of the Rothschild family.

'A large account, I suppose,' he said.

'Fairly large,' I whispered. 'I intend to place in this bank the sum of fifty-six dollars now and fifty dollars a month regularly.'

He got up, opened the door and called to the accountant.

'Mr Montgomery,' he said, in an unkindly loud voice, 'this gentleman is opening an account. He will place fifty-six dollars in it. Good morning.'

I stood up.

A big iron door stood open at the side of the room.

'Good morning,' I said, and walked into the safe.

'Come out,' said the manager coldly, and pointed me in the direction of a second door.

I went up to the accountant's desk and pushed the ball of money at him with a quick, sudden movement as if I were performing a sort of trick. My face was terribly pale.

'Here,' I said, 'put it in my account.' The sound of my voice seemed to mean, 'Let us do this painful thing while we still feel that we want to do it.'

He took the money and gave it to another clerk.

He made me write the sum on a piece of paper and sign my

★Pinkerton's: a well-known American firm of detectives.

67

name in a book. I no longer knew what I was doing. The bank seemed to swim before my eyes.

'Is it in the account?' I asked in a hollow, shaking voice.

'It is,' said the accountant.

'Then I want to write a cheque.'

My idea was to take out six dollars of it for my present use. Someone gave me a chequebook and someone else began telling me how to write it out. The people in the bank treated me like a man who owned millions of dollars, but was unwell. I wrote something on the cheque and pushed it towards the clerk. He looked at it.

'What! Are you taking it all out again?' he asked in surprise. Then I realized that I had written fifty-six dollars instead of six. I was too upset to explain my mistake. All the clerks had stopped writing to look at me.

I had to make a decision.

'Yes, the whole thing.'

'You wish to take your money out of the bank?'

'Every cent of it.'

'Are you not going to put any more in the account?' said the clerk, surprised.

'Never.'

A foolish hope came to me that they might think something had offended me while I was writing the cheque and that I had changed my mind. I made a useless attempt to look like a man with an extremely quick temper.

The clerk prepared to pay the money.

'How will you have it?' he said.

'What?'

'How will you have it?'

'Oh' – I understood his meaning and answered without even thinking about it – 'in fifty-dollar notes.'

He gave me a fifty-dollar note.

'And the six?' he asked coldly.

'In six-dollar notes,' I said.

He gave me six dollars and I rushed out.

As the big door swung behind me I heard the sound of laughter rising to the ceiling of the bank. Since then I no longer use a bank. I keep my money in my trouser pocket and my savings in silver dollars in a sock.

ACTIVITIES

Silas The Good

Before you read

1 Read the Introduction to this book.
   a What do all the stories have in common?
   b What do all the writers have in common?
2 Look at the Word List at the back of the book.
   a Find six words which refer to people.
   b Find three creatures that live on land or in water.
   c Find two different kinds of ground.
   d Find five emotional and/or physical reactions to a situation.
   e What is the connection between a berth, a landing stage and a steward?

While you read

3 Complete each sentence.
   a Uncle Silas works in a ....
   b There are golden flowers between the ....
   c Silas stops to eat at ....
   d The woman is carrying an ....
   e She thinks Uncle Silas is ....
   f He gives her a cupful of cold ....
4 Complete these sentences from the story with the correct endings, 1–7.
   a She took a real drink then, ...
   b He took his coat and ...   .
   c She took off her hat and ...   .
   d Somehow she stopped looking like a female and ...   .
   e Uncle Silas had drunk more in 80 years than ...   .
   f Except that her face was very red, she ...   .
   g The woman appeared to be a little excited, and ...   .
   1) held it on her knees.
   2) walked away as proudly as she had come.
   3) washing it round her mouth.

4) to everyone's embarrassment she talked a great deal.

5) became a woman.

6) there is water in the Thames.

7) spread it on the new earth above the grave.

After you read

5 Work with another student. Have this conversation.

    Student A: You are the woman in the churchyard. Explain to another passenger on the train about your meeting with Uncle Silas.

    Student B: You are the a passenger on the 2.45 train from Solbrook. Listen and ask questions.

Mabel

Before you read

6 In this story, a man and his girlfriend are soon going to meet again and marry after seven years apart. How do you think they are feeling? Why?

While you read

7 Circle the correct word or phrase in *italics* in each sentence.

  a The man at the club asks the writer if he would like a *sandwich / drink / game of cards*.

  b George is feeling *lost / happy / bored* without his wife.

  c The secretary says that Mabel is *strange / peculiar / unusual*.

  d When George went to meet Mabel from the ship, he suddenly felt *sick / angry / afraid*.

  e George decided he couldn't *marry / write to / avoid* Mabel.

  f In Singapore there was a *letter / telegram / package* waiting for him.

  g George realized that Mabel was *punishing / waiting for / following* him.

8 Number these places 1–8 in the order of George's route from Singapore.

Saigon .....   Manila .....   Cheng-Tu .....   Shanghai ..... / .....

Yokohama .....   Bangkok .....   Hong Kong .....

After you read

9 Explain:

    a Mabel's reaction to George's first letter;

    b what George then tried to do;

    c Mabel's reaction to what George was trying to do;

    d how George reacted when they met in Cheng-Tu;

    e how Mabel behaved when they met in Cheng-Tu.

The Barber's Uncle

Before you read

10 What do you think is the difference between a barber and a hairdresser?

While you read

11 Are these sentences right (✓) or wrong (✗)?

    a The writer has blond hair. .....

    b Huntingdon is a very rich man. .....

    c The boy realizes that there is a bird is in his hair
when it starts singing. .....

    d Aram is an experienced barber. .....

    e The boy and Aram drink tea together. .....

    f The boy thinks Aram is very wise and interesting. .....

12 Put these sentences about Uncle Misak and the tiger in the correct order, 1–8.

    a A wild tiger bit the head off Simon Perigord. .....

    b The tiger became hot and angry. .....

    c Uncle Misak fought for money. .....

    d Uncle Misak went to China. .....

    e The tiger bit off Uncle Misak's head. .....

    f Uncle Misak nearly died of hunger in Vienna. .....

    g Uncle Misak met an Arab man who worked in a
French travelling show. .....

    h The travelling show went to Persia. .....

13 The writer says of Uncle Misak's story that it is 'the sad story of every man alive.' Discuss what you think he might mean by this. Do you agree?

The Rocking-Horse Winner

Before you read

14 Do many children in your country have rocking-horses? Did you have one? What do you think the connection can be between the rocking-horse in this story and the idea of winning?

While you read

15 Choose the right answer (1–9) to each question.

  a Who does Paul's mother blame for the family's financial situation? .....

  b Where does Paul sit to find the secret of luck? .....

  c Who is Bassett? .....

  d What does Uncle Oscar talk to Paul about? .....

  e Who does Paul suggest could be partners? .....

  f Who looks after Paul's money? .....

  g Who does Paul want to give his money to? .....

  h Where does Paul's mother want to send him .....

  i What is Malabar? .....

  1) A horse.

  2) His mother.

  3) Paul's father.

  4) The gardener.

  5) On his rocking-horse.

  6) Uncle Oscar, Bassett and Paul.

  7) To the seaside.

  8) Bassett.

  9) Horse racing.

16 Why do you think Paul is such a strange child? Could his death have been prevented?

Springtime on the Menu

Before you read

17 Read this sentence from the story:
'Sarah was crying over the menu.'
   a Where do you think Sarah is at the time?
   b Why do you think she is crying?

While you read

18 Circle the correct words in italics to complete the sentences.
   a Sarah opens the world a little with a *typewriter / copy-typing*.
   b Schulenberg's is *an office / a restaurant*.
   c Sarah has an *agreement / argument* with Schulenberg's.
   d Schulenberg's send Sarah three *menus / meals* every day.
   e Sarah is in love with a *farmer / gardener*.
   f Walter put *flowers / grass* in her hair.
   g There are *dandelions / vegetables* on the new menu.

19 Who is speaking – Sarah (S) or Walter (W)?
   a 'New York is a rather large town.'   .....
   b 'I wrote to you.'   .....
   c 'Never got it!'   .....
   d 'He told me where you lived.'   .....

After you read

20 Explain how these are important to the story.
   the typewriter   Schulenberg's menu   dandelions

The Open Window

Before you read

21 What would you do if you wanted to get rid of an unwelcome visitor? List ways of dealing with people that you:
   a know well.
   b do not know well.

22 Who:

    a is upstairs when Mr Nuttel arrives? ....

    b has given him letters of introduction? ....

    c knows very little about Mrs Sappleton? ....

    d points to the French window? ....

    e wore a white coat? ....

    f sang to annoy Mrs Sappleton? ....

23 What:

    a have the men been shooting? ....

    b does Mr Nuttel talk about to change
       the subject? ....

    c is each of the three men carrying? ....

    d causes Mr Nuttel to run away? ....

    e does Mrs Sappleton think of Mr Nuttel? ....

    f does Vera say that Mr Nuttel is afraid of? ....

After you read

24 Work with another student. Have this conversation.

    Student A: You are Framton Nuttel. Tell your sister about your
               visit to Mrs Sappleton.

    Student B: You are Mr Nuttel's sister. Ask questions. Then tell Mr
               Nuttel what you think really happened.

The Income-Tax Man

Before you read

25 What taxes are paid in your country? What questions are people asked before they pay tax on their income?

While you read

26 Answer these questions with Yes or No:

    a Does the writer understand what the stranger's
       business is? .....

    b Does he think the stranger is honest? .....

    c Is the stranger surprised at the writer's income? .....

    d Does the stranger tell any of his own secrets? .....

e Is the writer happy with the contents of the envelope? .....

f Does he still respect the stranger? .....

g Does he pay all the tax that he should? .....

h Does he keep his own self-respect? .....

After you read

27 Work with another student. Have this conversation in the tax office.

Student A: You are the tax assessor. Interview the wealthy man from the story about his income for the year. You have his tax form in front of you.

Student B: You are the wealthy man in the story, and you intend to pay no tax. Answer the assessor's questions.

The Upper Berth

Before you read

28 Have you ever been on a long sea journey? If so, what did you like/dislike about it? If not, what do you think you would/would not enjoy?

While you read

29 Who is Brisbane talking about in these sentences?

the steward (S)   the doctor (D)   the captain (C)

a I shall never forget the expression on his face. .....

b I gave him a few coins there and then. .....

c He was a young man from the west of Ireland. .....

d His manner, as he spoke of the ship, was strange. .....

e He seemed very much annoyed at hearing that I knew of it. .....

f The result was that he got his money. .....

g He was not the man to be discouraged by a silly story. .....

h He was not hurt but he seemed hardly conscious. .....

i He took care of my broken arm and told me not to play with ghosts again. .....

30 Tell Brisbane's story from the point of view of the doctor.

My Bank Account

Before you read

31 Describe how bank accounts are opened in your country. How do you then put money in or take it out?

While you read

32 <u>Underline</u> the wrong word in each sentence and write the correct word.

a	The writer feels confident in a bank.	....
b	He wants to speak to the accountant.	....
c	The manager takes him to a public room.	....
d	The manager thinks he is a robber.	....
e	The writer walks into the cupboard.	....
f	He gives his money to the clerk.	....
g	After opening an account, he writes a letter.	....
h	From outside he can hear the sound of singing in the bank.	....
i	Now he keeps his savings in a pocket.	....

After you read

33 Act out a conversation between two bank clerks after the writer has left the bank. One of you feels sorry for him; the other one doesn't.

Writing

34 Choose one of the stories and explain why you did or did not enjoy it.

35 Compare George and Mabel's relationship with Walter and Sarah's.

36 What effects do the lies of Silas and young Vera have on their listeners? What would have happened in each case if they had not lied?

37 Which of these stories do you think could be the starting point for a film? Why? What would be the biggest difficulty in filming it?

38 Six of the nine stories are told in the first person (*I*). Why do you think the writers chose to do this, instead of using the third person (*He/She*)? What are the disadvantages of first person writing?

39 Compare the style of 'Springtime on the Menu' with 'The Rocking-Horse Winner'. Which do you think is more enjoyable to read? Why?

40 Describe the personality of either Paul in 'The Rocking-Horse Winner' or Brisbane in 'The Upper Berth'.

41 All these stories were written in, or are set in, the first half of the twentieth century. Choose one of the stories and re-write it, bringing it up to date.

42 Imagine that you are Vera, in 'The Open Window'. Some years later you meet Framton Nuttel's sister. Explain to her why you lied to her brother. Start like this: *I was just fifteen years old, and life in the country bored me. When your brother* . . . .

43 After the Kamtschatka returns to port ('The Upper Berth'), the captain has to send a report to the ship's owners. Write his report, explaining why room 105 is no longer available to passengers.

Answers for the Activities in this book are available from the Penguin Readers website. A free Activity Worksheet is also available from the website. Activity Worksheets are part of the Penguin Teacher Support Programme, which also includes Progress Tests and Graded Reader Guidelines. For more information, please visit: www.penguinreaders.com.

WORD LIST

account (n) an arrangement that allows you to keep your money in a bank and take it out when you need it; a description of an event or process. An **accountant** keeps and checks financial records.

anxiety (n) the feeling of being very worried about something

assessor (n) someone who calculates the value or cost of something

barber (n) a man who cuts men's hair

bearer (n) someone who carries something

berth (n) a bed on a ship

bog (n) an area of low, wet, muddy ground

cart (n) an open vehicle that is pulled by a horse

clay (n) a type of heavy, sticky earth that can be used for making pots

consul (n) a government official who lives in a foreign country and helps people from his or her own country who are living or visiting there

damp (n/adj) water in the air or in walls that makes things slightly wet

dandelion (n) a wild plant with a bright yellow flower

delicate (adj) easily becomes ill or damaged

determined (adj) to have a strong desire to do something, so you won't let anyone stop you

duck (n) a common water bird with short legs, used for its meat, eggs and soft feathers

feverishly (adj) in a state of great excitement or worry

holy (adj) connected with religion

landing stage (n) a wooden platform that people walk along when they go to or leave a boat

oyster (n) a type of shellfish that can be eaten cooked or uncooked

relief (n) a feeling of comfort when something frightening, worrying or painful has ended or hasn't happened

telegram (n) a message sent using electrical signals

rate (n) the amount of a payment

reasonable (adj) fair and sensible

rocking-horse (n) a wooden horse for children that moves backwards and forwards when you sit on it

shilling (n) an old British coin; there were twenty shillings in one pound

spring (n) a twisted piece of metal that returns to its previous shape after it has been pressed down

steward (n) a man who looks after passengers' needs on a ship

trade (n/v) business activity, especially the activity of buying and selling

tremble (v) to shake slightly, in a way that you can't control

worm (n) a long, thin creature with no bones and no legs that lives in the ground